Insider Outsider is a smart, candid, and transparent reflection on the state of modern white evangelicalism in America. Bryan Loritts implores us to see and embrace the fullness and simplicity of the good news and to be brave enough to reject any counterfeits in the process.

DR. KORIE EDWARDS, associate professor of sociology at
The Ohio State University and author of *The Elusive Dream*

The first time Bryan Loritts preached at our church, my eight-year-old daughter said, "Dad, you should preach more like that guy." Bryan has an ability to communicate truth with a poignancy that challenges the seasoned believer and an accessibility that engages the eight-year-old. *Insider Outsider* is filled with provocative questions that at times made me squirm but need to be asked. We in the white evangelical community need to understand what is in the hearts of our brothers and sisters of color, and Bryan helps us see them from his unique vantage points. He serves up strong medicine on a bed of humor and personal illustration and with a blanket of genuine pastoral warmth. Prepare to be challenged, enlightened, and encouraged.

J.D. GREEAR, PHD, pastor of The Summit Church, Raleigh-Durham,
North Carolina, and president of the Southern Baptist Convention

If ever there was a time for this book, it is *now*. Bryan Loritts's voice in this critical conversation is informed, winsome, and challenging. Reading this with an open mind, a humble heart, and an intentional spirit truly may move us toward God's kingdom on earth.

NANCY ORTBERG, CEO of Transforming the Bay with Christ

The diligent outside scholarship and inside insight required to make substantive commentary on sensitive issues such as race, with equal impact in both spiritual and social arenas, are laudable. Bryan Loritts again proves he's more than up for the task. We are edified and indeed rendered "woke" to some important concepts that have the potential to be game changers in this fraught epoch of the church's calling. The battle for understanding and true equality surely includes what Bryan
spiritual insight inspired and informed

KIRK

Being an African American serving in a predominantly Anglo denomination, I know firsthand how critical it is for different races to work together to accomplish God's will in the church today. *Insider Outsider* is a must-read for those of us who desire the church to look and act like God's church.

FRED LUTER, pastor of Franklin Avenue Baptist Church, New Orleans, and former president of the Southern Baptist Convention

Bryan Loritts is one of the most intelligent people I've ever met. He is also deeply committed to Jesus, the church, and the gospel. This book will challenge you and make you uncomfortable, just like a good personal trainer does. If we are humble enough to listen to and love one another, *Insider Outsider* has the capacity to truly make a difference.

DR. DERWIN L. GRAY, lead pastor of Transformation Church and author of *The High Definition Leader*

Insider Outsider is biblically informed, intellectually brilliant, and desperately needed. Bryan Loritts's clear prophetic voice stands in the gap for generations of voiceless ethnic-minority Christians in America. With pastoral sensitivity and unwavering boldness, he calls Christ's church to embrace real diversity by challenging us to reevaluate our worldview, repent of our sin, and embrace the rich diversity God has created for us, his people. This book is a must-read for all Christians.

PASTOR DOUG LOGAN JR., director of the Diversity Initiative and codirector of Church in Hard Places, Acts 29 network; author of *On the Block*

Bryan Loritts is masterful in utilizing the power of story and an astute understanding of the times to unearth the darkness in the current culture. *Insider Outsider* is a must-read for those looking for poignant direction on hope for change and those aspiring to grow in unity.

CHRIS DAVIS, lead pastor of Redemption Church San Francisco

Insider Outsider

Insider Outsider

MY JOURNEY AS A STRANGER IN WHITE
EVANGELICALISM AND MY HOPE FOR US ALL

Bryan Loritts

ZONDERVAN

Insider Outsider
Copyright © 2018 by Bryan Loritts

Requests for information should be addressed to:
Zondervan, *3900 Sparks Dr. SE, Grand Rapids, Michigan 49546*

ISBN 978-0-310-34503-9 (softcover)

ISBN 978-0-310-35538-0 (audio)

ISBN 978-0-310-34500-8 (ebook)

Published in association with the literary agency of Wolgemuth & Associates, Inc.

Cover design: Catherine Casalino
Interior design: Kait Lamphere

First printing July 2018 / Printed in the United States of America

*To that little conference room
peering over Poplar Avenue
and all the aspiring leaders trained there.
May you never lose hope.*

Contents

Multiethnic Sharecropping

Kaepernicked

Scouting Jackie

Trumped

"Gay" and Other Labels

A Love Supreme

Foreword

In 1808, David Barrow wrote a biblical attack on race-based slavery with the formidable title *Involuntary, unmerited, perpetual, absolute, hereditary slavery examined on the principles of nature, reason, justice, policy and scripture*. It did not accomplish what he hoped. Historian Mark Noll wrote that the great theological crisis of the Civil War was the inability to distinguish between slavery and racism, which meant that even after the war was over and slavery was abolished, "systemic racism continued unchecked as the great moral anomaly in supposedly Christian America."[1]

And so it goes.

I suspect that, for many white readers, listening to Bryan Loritts in *Insider Outsider* will illumine corners of our world, our churches, and our minds that are often unexamined and perhaps even unimagined. Pastor Loritts is a remarkably gifted preacher, the son of a gifted preacher, who knows the world of white evangelicalism and brings to it what W. E. B. Du Bois called "double-consciousness, this sense of always looking at one self through the eyes of others," a vision that Du Bois said could be a great, though painful, gift if only white America would really receive it.[2]

Pastor Loritts distinguishes between white evangelicals and "white evangelicalism," a subculture shaped by an agenda of whiteness that sees the world through a lens of whiteness so pervasive it is often unrecognized, that equates "whiteness" with "normal." So, for instance, "black preaching" is emotive or visceral or call-and-response; "white preaching" isn't even a recognizable phrase; it's just "preaching." He asks why black preachers always feel the pressure to bend in the direction of a white congregation's expectation, while white preachers generally feel the freedom to "be themselves," even in the (remote) possibility they might preach to an African-American congregation. In these and a hundred other ways, we reveal who "owns"' the place and who does not.

Decades of research have shown that implicit racial bias is epidemic. A survey in the *Journal of Alcohol and Drug Education* asked respondents to envision and describe a drug user: 95 percent described an African American, although in fact only 15 percent of drug users were African American and the vast majority were white.[3] Research further shows that such biases lead to discriminatory actions. Paul said that sin "dwells in [our] members" (Romans 7:23); this is true of the sin of racism. And good intentions alone (even when present) will not deliver us.

The election of Donald Trump in 2016—who propagated a "birther myth" to discredit Barack Obama and received 81 percent of the vote of white evangelicals but was in single digits with African Americans (who are more likely to be "evangelical" in their theology than Caucasians)—has raised deeply troubling questions. *Insider Outsider* notes that the troublesome word in the slogan "make America great again" is *again*. In which year was it, exactly, that America was great? 1753? 1853? 1953? To which year would our brothers and sisters of color want to return?

The way to shalom is not backward. And yet disturbing trends continue to point in that direction. Legal scholar Michelle Alexander points out that the United States has the highest incarceration rates in the world, that the racial dimension of mass incarceration is its most striking feature, and that in some states black men have been admitted to prison on drug charges at rates twenty to fifty times greater than white men.[4] Bryan Stevenson has noted that Alabama, in the buckle of the Bible Belt, still had a ban on interracial marriage in the twenty-first century.[5]

The voice of this book seeks to be—as evangelical voices in our day generally do—"gospel-centered." But the question must be raised:

"Whose gospel?" The gospel Jesus preached (see Mark 1:14–15) announced the availability through him of life in the kingdom of God, the range of God's effective will. And God's will includes definite parameters about dignity, equality, social structures, and economic fairness. Jesus came, notes Yale philosopher Nicholas Wolterstorff, as "the Spirit-anointed servant who proclaims the coming of justice."[6] And any account of "gospel" that ignores the social content of "God's effective will" is not the gospel that Jesus proclaimed.

This is not a book without hope. But it's not my place to speak of hope. Hope can come too glibly to the tongue for those who have sat at the table of privilege too easily for too long. So it may be helpful for the reader to start with a willingness to bear discomfort. Any hope worth having is willing to start there, and stay there.

John Ortberg

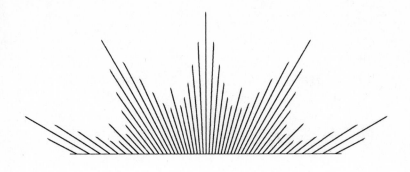

An Evangelical
Eulogy

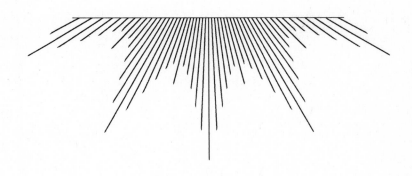

CHAPTER 1

Listen

While the fires of the Great Awakening were enflaming souls up and down the eastern seaboard of America, a slave had found himself enraptured by the preaching of George Whitefield. Alone in the confines of his quarters, he decided to pay the theatrical gospel preacher the ultimate form of flattery—namely, impersonation. Unbeknownst to him, standing outside the door was his master, totally enamored by what his property was doing. *Others had to see this*, he thought.

So he sent out a call to some of his friends, poured a few glasses of whiskey, and summoned his slave for an encore performance. The sight of a slave trying to pull off a British accent overwhelmed them with laughter, but in the midst of doubling over, something happened—and it wasn't the whiskey. An eerie sense of seriousness hovered over the room, as these men began to contemplate the sobriety of the cross. The gospel began to eke out of this vaudevillian performance. Things were no longer funny.

This story presents far more than sermonic fodder for the potency of the gospel. I have felt like this slave during my sojourn in the land of white evangelicalism. Many of my invitations to speak to majority white audiences come because of my ability to strike safe homiletical chords also hit by our modern-day George Whitefields. In the infancy of my ministry, I found myself simply parroting the words of these well-known white evangelicals without wrestling with these truths before embracing them as mine.

My imitation of them earned me entrée to white audiences, much like what happened with this slave. On more than a few occasions, I have been told by my white hosts how boring white preachers can be and how entertaining black ones are. I've been asked by the white leaders who invited me to speak at their event if I'm going to whoop, and if I am going to "bring it." These questions inspire a gladiatorial neurosis of sorts in which I want to scream, "I do not entertain."

And as I've stood before a sea of white faces throughout my ministry, I have wrestled with feelings of belonging, as this slave undoubtedly did as he took his stand before his Communion-consuming gathering. And yet, through all of this, the gospel somehow does its thing. Unconfined by human brokenness, the foolishness of the good news leaks out across oppression, racism, and bad motives. My nana had it right when she said, "God hits straight licks with crooked sticks."

The history of evangelicalism in America begins with the Puritans. Even a cursory reading of their writings and knowledge of their history will reveal a deep passion for God and an honest attempt to live by the Scriptures. Their books have a unique quality of enflaming the soul. (I've read them. I know.)

Yet our nation's evangelical ancestors had feet of clay and were deeply misguided in a plethora of ways, especially when it came to race. Many owned slaves. For example, Cotton Mather had slaves included in his compensation package when he became the pastor of a church.[7] He even gave his slave a biblical name—Onesimus—and referred to him as an "it."

Furthermore, many Puritans played a complicit role in crafting a culture that was hostile to people of color, seeing and treating them as less than people. Known for their robust soteriology, theirs was a flawed anthropology, and all of this was exacted from seats of religious, social, and political power.

This historical context unveils the truth that evangelicalism and white evangelicalism happen to be at least four-hundred-or-so-year-old conjoined twins who have never been separated in their lives.

The recorded history of evangelicalism in America began with white people, and because white Christians have historically possessed seats of power, white evangelicalism has become the standard operating system by which the authenticity of one's Christianity and convictions is vetted. The long and winding story of white evangelicalism is one of *oppression*.

But there I go, using that term again. What do I mean by it? Brother George Whitefield is helpful. If there had been a Mount Rushmore of evangelicals during his time, Whitefield's cherubic image most certainly would have been etched upon it. Blessed with stunning gifts of oratory and a sincere heart for Christ, Whitefield saw many come to faith in Jesus. Like all of us, however, Whitefield was complicated, an amalgamation of genius and idiocy, righteousness and evil. It was because of the lobbying of George Whitefield that Georgia finally legalized slavery.

Why did this famed evangelical take the posture of a little child pulling annoyingly on the hem of Georgia trustee, General James Oglethorpe, begging him to permit slavery? Whitefield noticed that in the Bible, God makes a clarion call for people to care for orphans, and so moved by the Word, Whitefield summoned all of his evangelical powers to convince the leaders of the colony of Georgia to provide a safe haven where black people could be bought and sold, thus allowing him to establish a plantation model to fund his care for white orphans. The one who set the captives free at the same time kept them in bondage, and his justification for his fallacies was God's Word.

George Whitefield had fallen victim to allowing his particular time and ethnicity to color his hermeneutics. Little did this great evangelical preacher know that his was a theology done in white. The real problem was not that it was colored in white, but that he didn't see it. Pete Scazzero observes that when a person walks into a room, they bring a whole lot more than just themselves. Their parents, siblings, and important influencers come into the room as well.[8] For we have all been shaped by our upbringing.

The same is true when we approach the biblical text. Any good hermeneutics professor will tell you we bring so much more than our Greek and Hebrew analytics to the text; we also bring our ethnicity (and other lenses such as gender, class, and culture).

As a black man, I pause when I see that Jesus was taken to Africa as a baby for refuge (Matthew 2:13–18). My blackness will not allow me to gloss over the Ethiopian man whom Philip cozies up to in Acts 8:26–39, or the fact that Moses, the legendary liberator and lawgiver, marries a black woman (Exodus 2:21). I rejoice when I see God chastising Moses's siblings for their failure to truly embrace his interracial marriage (Numbers 12:1). I nurse a low-grade fever over the master-slave passages, wanting Paul to be far more vociferous and denounce these institutions (1 Corinthians 7:21–24; Ephesians 6:5–9; Colossians 3:22–4:1). And I see the irony of God calling an oppressed Jew—Peter—to carry the gospel to the oppressor Gentile Roman soldier named Cornelius (Acts 10). My blackness cannot be disrobed as I engage God's Word.

Neither can one's whiteness, and I am grateful for that. Theology must always be done in community within the context of our unique biases, both as a means to enrich and to be challenged. But what makes white evangelicalism problematic is that it has never truly submitted itself as simply *one of many* perspectives within the buffet of American Christianity.

When I teach preaching at a seminary level, one of the first exercises I have my students do is to define for me what "black preaching" and "black theology" are. Hands of all different colors go up. Then I ask students to define "white preaching" and "white theology." The pause is palpable. Moments of awkward silence ensue—a quiet admission that they have never entertained this question before.

It's awfully hard to define what one has normalized and main-streamed. It's like asking fish to describe water. This is the challenge we face with white evangelicalism. It has been the very water of main-stream American life for more than four hundred years. It has been the home team. White evangelicalism has not only brought its perspective, but it has historically done so from a position of religious, cultural, and political power. Left unchecked, this power has morphed into ugly periods of oppression and tyranny.

I was in the store the other day when I came across an Asian woman who was trying to explain herself to the proprietor. Her accent was heavy. She sounded like she was from some faraway place—perhaps Vietnam. Wherever she was from, it was clear that America was not her country of origin. Her English was labored and slow, like a child taking her first steps. I watched as the proprietor talked in loud, slow tones, like the parent of the child taking the first steps minus the jubilation. He was clearly annoyed. Before I could give any measured thought to the situation, I also found myself perturbed, since I too had a question for the proprietor and this customer was slowing me down. *Clearly this woman isn't smart*, I thought.

Now these foolish assumptions were made within the span of seconds, and all because she didn't talk like me. Yes, she spoke English, but her thick accent wasn't like mine. In fact, do I even have an accent? I know I do, but I never think about it in this way. To me, I just talk normal, and if you don't talk normal the way I talk normal, then you're probably dumb or "less than."

We tend to label people who have an obvious accent. My friends are surprised when I tell them I grew up in Atlanta, because I don't talk Southern. My mother is from Philadelphia, and she thought Southern accents were ridiculous, so she forbade any semblance of them in her house. Saying "y'all" would get us banished to our bedroom for the evening. When I detect a New York accent, I automatically think that person is rude and arrogant. When I hear a Midwestern accent, I think, *She probably calls her grandmother "Grandma" and is from a blue-collar family.* A California accent on a young person means he or she probably smokes weed. There, I said it. But I for sure don't have an accent! I just talk normal while I wonder why everyone doesn't talk normal like I do.

The problem with white evangelicalism is not that it has an accent, but that it fails to see the ethnic theological accent it possesses. This glaucoma of sorts leads white evangelicals to normalize their hermeneutical biases while wielding them as a tool of oppression where anyone who doesn't see it the way they do tends to be castigated, ostracized, blogged about, or ignored. Because white evangelicalism is based on assumption, you will not find a president or CEO of white evangelicalism, just as you won't find the head of the American Accent Academy. Instead, white evangelicalism gets annoyed with those who do theology in Vietnamese or with any other kind of accent, assuming they are not as smart, when instead the reverse is probably true. I only speak one language, while the woman in the store speaks at least two.

Now if indeed this woman is a native of Vietnam and I were to visit her country and find myself in a store trying to leverage the few words I do know in her mother tongue, who would look unintelligent then? Accents tend to be judged by those who represent the home team.

White evangelicalism has been the theological home team within Christianity since day one. Everyone else has been a guest in her fields. Many slaves were taught the accent of Reformed theology from their evangelical masters. Native Americans were exhorted by recent European immigrants to depart from many of their cultural customs in exchange for a Jesus who looked and acted European. And anyone who has studied the history of missions can attest to the oppressive nature of white evangelicalism, where in a myriad of instances she has led the "uncivilized" to faith while seeking to disrobe the new converts of their cultural expressions. Thus, the problem is not just that our white siblings do theology in white and have normalized their conclusions; it's that they've done it from the box seat of power within their own stadium.

This book aims to challenge the *accent* of white evangelicalism, not the *language* she speaks. By this, I am highlighting a dichotomy between substance and form. But herein lies the problem: it is what happens when accents get elevated to the level of language. This is the historic error that white evangelicalism has made, which is why it must be eulogized.

As we set out together, a few things will be helpful. First, it needs to be said there is a difference between being a white evangelical and white evangelicalism. Ray Chang, who serves as a ministry associate in Wheaton College's chaplain's office, proves helpful here. He defines evangelicalism as "(1) a movement of gospel centrality, focused on the primacy of scripture and justification by faith that emerged from the reformation, (2) a modern movement within Protestantism marked by [historian David] Bebbington's quadrilateral of Biblicism, Crucicentrism, Conversionism, and Activism." He goes on to define white evangelicalism as "a segment of modern evangelicalism that is led and shaped by a cultural agenda defined by whiteness."[9] In an epoch where, for many, *white* has become a four-letter word, let it be said that all must value and cherish our white familia. The blood of Jesus Christ has bonded us together, and to allow ourselves to be handcuffed by the armlets of suspicion, bitterness, and unforgiveness is out of step with the gospel (Matthew 18:21–35). But *white evangelicalism* is another thing. The former has to do with a person, the latter a system that has long oppressed.

This is a caustic statement that places the burden of proof upon me. So how do I show you this? While one's perception of facts is debatable, their experience is not. The best way I can expose the monarchy of white evangelicalism in America is to pull you along in my journey. As a second-generation preacher whose African-American father is well trafficked within the halls of white evangelicalism, I have a unique perch, for I have likewise followed in his steps. White evangelicalism has opened doors for me, but it has also almost dismantled my ethnic scaffolding.

In my pilgrimage, she has embraced my face while muting my voice. This was the fiery trial of the woman known as "The Voice"— Whitney Houston. When she stuck to the script handed to her by the powers that lorded it over her and sang pop, she sold well north of a hundred million albums and became universally embraced (while booed famously by many African Americans at one of our award shows). Yet the moment she expressed a desire to step out of that box and return to her black church roots, which gave birth to R&B, she bumped up against the impenetrable glass ceiling. Whitney's travails represent a universal blues for people of color laboring under white ownership. To be fully embraced within the world of white evangelicalism demands that we minister in the genre of pastoral pop. But the moment one of us steps out of that box and begins to hit other notes, we become aware of the proverbial glass ceiling.

What follows is my attempt to expose and lovingly smash this ceiling. These reflections are not meant to be debated or blogged about, but to be discussed and shared with someone who speaks in a different hermeneutical accent than yours. Yes, may we converse in the language of Jesus and orthodox love, but my hope is that *Insider Outsider* emboldens us to do so in our own ethnically interpretive tongue.

CHAPTER 2

An Invitation to
Life Together

The slain corpse of Michael Brown has decimated the myth that we live in a post-racial society. The election of our nation's first African-American president did not end racism. In many ways, we witnessed a fresh proliferation of conflicts between people of color and whites, the powerless and the powerful. In the aftermath of Brown's demise, there have been riots in his hometown, as well as on social media. In the Christian community, the commentary has likewise been combustible, as one side has appealed to the "facts" of the case— Michael Brown had just stolen some cigars and could very well have been the aggressor—and the other side has spoken out of a deep well of hurt, dug for more than four hundred years with the shovels of racism and institutionalized segregation, where the value of a black life was on a par with that of a horse. So as Michael Brown's body lay abandoned for hours on a street in Ferguson, Missouri, like some run-over possum or deer, it's more than understandable that African Americans began to wonder, "What exactly is the value of a black life?"

If you are looking for objectivity from my hand as I write, in many ways you will not find it. I am a follower of Jesus Christ who happens to be an African American, and because of this, there is a cultural filter by which I interpret the Michael Browns, Alton Sterlings, and Trayvon

Martins of the world. This is what I mean by *hermeneutic*—it is a way we interpret the world. I have one, and so do you.

African Americans have often been drawn to the nation of Israel, seeing in the ancient Jews parallels of hope. It was Dr. Martin Luther King Jr., on the eve of his assassination, who in his final speech likened himself to Moses, and the African-American experience to the sojourn of Israel. On the other hand, if one is affluent and white, it will be hard for them to immediately see the need to engage in justice, since this well-to-do narrative is triumphalistic and diminishes the realities of unjust systems and structures. Many Eastern cultures pick up on the communal dimensions of Scripture, while we in the West have a hard time seeing these things, being held captive by a culture steeped in rampant individualism. We all have a way of seeing the Bible.

On one level, I have a cultural hermeneutic. Reading the stories about the death of black bodies by white police officers takes me back to the killings of Emmett Till in 1955, Medgar Evers in 1963, Dr. Martin Luther King Jr. in 1968, and Oscar Grant in 2009 (Fruitvale Station). These men were cut down in the prime of their lives by whites (Emmett Till was fourteen when he died). What's more, Emmett, Medgar, Martin, and Oscar are but a few in a long history of African Americans who have been unjustly killed at the hands of our white brothers. As if that's not enough, in many cases, their killers were never brought to justice, and if they were, it was a long time coming. So, for example, when I see Michael Brown's corpse amid reports that he was shot by a representative of both the historic (white) and vocational (police) power structures of our country, I hope you will find it more than understandable if I cry foul. I, as a black man, find it impossible not to flinch at present circumstances, given the injustices of the past.

Over the years, I've been challenged by white evangelicals to just get over it. Their refusal to try to see things from my ethnically different perspective is a subtle, stinging form of racist oppression. What's more, it hinders true Christian unity and fellowship within the beloved body of Christ.

When a man and a woman get married, two narratives and sets of experiences, along with worldviews, collide. Imagine if your wife had previously been abused in such a way that impacted your intimacy with her. I don't think a simple "you should just get over it" approach would work.

Neither do I think that her outbursts over the Harvey Weinsteins of the world should provoke exasperation in which you exhale, "Is everything *always* about sexual assault with you?" Nor would it be sufficient to immediately appeal to the facts and say, "But I'm not the person who did it, so let's move on." If you truly loved her and wanted to journey with her to health and intimacy, you would do all you could to understand her story and journey, to try in some way to incarnate her pain and pilgrimage. This is the way forward into oneness.

We will never experience true Christian unity when one ethnicity demands of another that we keep silent about our pain and travails. The way forward is not an appeal to the facts as a first resort, but an attempt to get inside each other's skin as best as we can to feel what they feel and to seek to understand it. Tragedies such as the Michael Brown shooting in Ferguson are like MRIs that reveal the hurt that still lingers, and the chasm that exists between ethnicities can only be traversed if we move past facts and get into feelings.

The communication pyramid offers a revolutionary paradigm in our journey to understanding.[10] Basically, there are five levels of communication: (1) cliché, (2) facts, (3) opinions, (4) feelings, and (5) transparency, with *cliché* representing the shallowest form of communication and *transparency* the deepest. When something is troubling my bride, she will often come to me with level 4 (feelings), but when I stay in lawyer land at level 2, this is never a recipe for intimacy. I am not denying facts, but I've had to learn the hard way that if I am to experience oneness with my bride, I must drop down to level 4 in an attempt to understand, before I resurface to level 2. Facts are a first and last resort in a court of law, but when it comes to human relationships, let us first stop and feel before we go to facts.

Herein lies the problem. When racial incidents happen, people of color typically rush to feelings (level 4 on the communication pyramid), while many of our white siblings stay at level 2—appealing to facts. This is not the path to multiethnic empathy and harmony. Before we sort through the facts, we must first learn to listen to and feel with one another.

This book represents level 4 communication. The issues are not meant to be sparred over on the landscape of one's social media page, but to be processed and engaged across ethnic lines at some dinner table. To wage a war over the veracity of my experience would represent not only the absence of progress, but also a moonwalking of sorts away from the goal. In a word, it would be heartbreaking. *Insider Outsider* is an invitation to listen so that we may experience what Dietrich Bonhoeffer calls "life together."[11]

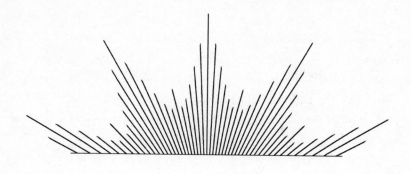

Higher
Learning

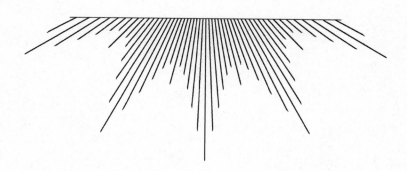

CHAPTER 3

School of Origins

I am no novice when it comes to white evangelicalism. From birth, I have made its acquaintance. Both of my parents are black and could not be more different. My father grew up in New Jersey and comes from a long lineage extending back to pre-emancipation days, where the men in his direct line loved Jesus and never divorced their wives. Mother is from the inner-city bowels of North Philadelphia, where there was no such thing as a man who married a Williams (her maiden name) and stayed with her for any significant period of time. My father came to faith at his black church in Plainfield, New Jersey—a Church of God church. Mother met Jesus at an aging, white Presbyterian church in North Philadelphia and sealed the deal at a white camp in the Poconos in the late 1950s. Their paths would collide in college at one of the strongholds for white evangelicalism, a school steeped in classic dispensationalism with very white, middle-class views of the kingdom, but I'm getting ahead of myself.

A few years after they wed, I came into the world on February 11, 1973—my father's birthday. My advent into the world was just a few short years after Dr. King was assassinated. His death marked a significant moment in our nation's history, as riots erupted in urban centers across the nation. Like being caught ill-prepared in a sudden rainstorm, the death of Martin Luther King Jr. left a pervasive sense of vulnerability among my tribe.

But there were also flashes of hopefulness. If major governmental gains had been made by King and the movement, the next frontier was the heart. It's here where minority evangelicals occupying space among white evangelicals asked if this was our moment. It's here where our attention turned to a black Jesus-loving man from the streets of Harlem named Tom Skinner. Tom was a voice crying in the wilderness—one of the first minority preachers with a broad multiethnic platform to speak truth to power as he called for a return to a holistic gospel that wedded our vertical relationship with Christ and our horizontal relationship with one another—and all of the glorious justice implications that entails. One cannot possibly understand evangelicalism in America without significant pause to peer over the life and ministry of this chocolate giant. Every person of color in evangelicalism owes him a debt of gratitude.

My father and Tony Evans (among others) were the spiritual progeny of Tom Skinner. The two were bound to become close—so close that my dad and Dr. Evans joined forces to plant the Oak Cliff Bible Fellowship in Dallas, Texas, in the mid-1970s. Not long into our time in Dallas, Dad felt the call to become an evangelist, and so he accepted the offer to work for what was then called Campus Crusade for Christ (now Cru), and we moved to Atlanta in the late 1970s. It was here, around the age of five, that my impressions of Christianity began to form and take shape.

I'm often asked by young minority leaders who aspire to engage in multiethnic ministry how I manage to relate so well across various ethnicities and cultures. Without hesitation, I point to my upbringing. My parents' work with CCC (Campus Crusade for Christ) immersed them in the front lines of white evangelicalism. Yet we belonged to an all-black church in the heart of Atlanta. And the schools I attended were split right down the middle, a direct result of mandated busing and its aftershocks. So a typical week for me was popping into my dad's office, where he was the only black man in charge of just about an all-white staff (if memory serves me right, two black women served there as well).

I spent Sundays at our no-central-air, all-black church, fanning myself with a wooden stick that had a piece of cardboard stapled to it—with a picture of Dr. King on one side and an advertisement for a funeral home on the other side. *Quite appropriate*, I thought. I felt as though I was going to die.

At that time, my school was fifty-fifty black and white. My childhood friends were a multiethnic cohort of sorts, with names like Dante, Eugene, Steve, Jeremy, Shondra, and Megan. In the ironic sovereignty of God, I was being shaped to be a multiethnic leader, but white evangelicalism would stand in the way.

CHAPTER 4

The Dark Side of Contextualization

I always knew I wanted to be a preacher, and I think a part of the reason is that it was all I was exposed to as I grew up. My father is a great preacher, and he was one of the few black preachers I knew who preached in just as many white arenas as minority ones. I would often tag along. My earliest memories are sitting on the front pew of some church, feet dangling off the edge too short to touch the ground, and being mesmerized as Dad preached. What a preacher!

But it's here where my first pangs with white evangelicalism would emerge. I would query Dad as to why he was so passionate at the black church—yelling, banging his hand on the pulpit, loosening his tie, wiping sweat from his forehead, and taking huge swallows of water—but was incredibly subdued in the white church. It seemed as if he had multiple personalities. Christianity calls this *contextualization*. W. E. B. Du Bois calls it something else:

> It is a peculiar sensation, this double-consciousness, this sense of always looking at one's self through the eyes of others, of measuring one's soul by the tape of a world that looks on in amused contempt and pity. One ever feels his two-ness,—an American, a Negro; two souls, two thoughts, two unreconciled strivings; two

warring ideals in one dark body, whose dogged strength alone keeps it from being torn asunder.

The history of the American Negro is the history of this strife,—this longing to attain self-conscious manhood, to merge his double self into a better and truer self. In this merging he wishes neither of the older selves to be lost. He would not Africanize America, for America has too much to teach the world and Africa. He would not bleach his Negro soul in a flood of white Americanism, for he knows that Negro blood has a message for the world. He simply wishes to make it possible for a man to be both a Negro and an American without being cursed and spit upon by his fellows, without having the doors of Opportunity closed roughly in his face.[12]

This is by far Du Bois's most popular quote because it resonates so deeply, touching a universal chord we people of color feel. Contextualization is biblical (see 1 Corinthians 9:19–23), but what Du Bois points to is the psychology of the minority "contextualizer." Because white evangelicalism has always treated us as a guest in her house, minorities never truly feel at home. We feel, as Du Bois calls it, this "two-ness." We are compelled to contextualize, not so much to reach the audience, but to be embraced and validated.

In order to wrap our arms around this, one must ask why this is not a two-way street. I'm not sure how much preaching you've heard, if any at all, but I doubt you've heard more preaching than me. At best, I can count on three fingers the number of white evangelicals who have contextualized their preaching to fit the norms of minorities in their churches and spaces. With very few exceptions, it's hard to find a white preacher whose normal mode of speaking is more conversational and subdued, who when he comes to a minority environment that is used to a more emotive and passionate oratory bends his norm to meet the expectations of this crowd in an authentic, well-intentioned way. Historically white evangelicalism has oppressed people of color by failing to accommodate their methodologies to speak on a level where they can truly receive the gospel. As long as contextualization remains a one-way street, it is racist oppression, and it must die.

And yet this conversation does not go far enough. We must ask an even more invasive question: Why do minority preachers feel the need to contextualize in white environments, while with us they do not? That is the question. I can only tell you what I have felt, along with some of the shared sentiments from my minority colleagues. Often we struggle with an internal angst as people of color who ascend the pulpit to be accepted and validated, to prove our belonging to whites. Like the maid Aibeleen in *The Help* who is coaching the young child Mae Mobley, we people of color in the preaching moment want to show, "We are smart." So we contextualize. We tone things down. We are careful with our words. We make sure our theology is sound. We don't want to ruffle the feathers, so we stay safe. Are these things bad in and of themselves? Of course not, but what I'm getting at is the motive, the driving force, behind the contextualizing.

Now in some sense, who doesn't want to feel accepted in the preaching moment, no matter the context? Yet, the question does remain, why does it appear as if our white siblings do not have that same angst in the sermonic moment? Their refusal to take any steps toward us in their rhetoric or presentation shows the oppressive normalization of white evangelicalism, where its dastardly message is, "You bend to us; we will never bend to you."

CHAPTER 5

Bible School Initiation

When I was seventeen, a tragic event happened. My dear friend Craig Tarleton collapsed and died of a heart attack while running around the track of our high school. He was just seventeen. Prior to his death, I felt an uncommon urge to share my faith with him. Every day, I'd walk into the chemistry class we shared, and it seemed as if God was grabbing me by the collar of my Members Only jacket, begging me to talk about my faith with Craig. But I gave in to thoughts of rejection and told God I'd get to it later. Well, later never came.

So there I was, sitting at his funeral on the outskirts of our little town just south of Atlanta, and for the first time, I was confronted with my own mortality. At seventeen, you never think about death. All thoughts and impulses are present or future. Where will I go to college? How did I do on the SAT? What will I major in? What will I do with my life? Will she say yes to me if I ask her to the prom? It's never, "Tomorrow is not promised to you." I made a decision as I sat at my departed friend's funeral to get serious about my faith.

If you tell black church folk you want to preach, they're going to want to know when you got the call. In my tribe, preaching is not something you decide to do—like which restaurant you'll eat at—but it is something you are mystically called to and compelled to do. Like fire shut up in Jeremiah's bones (Jeremiah 20:9) is the call to preach in the black experience. It was there, a few feet away from my friend's casket, that I gave in and decided to embrace God's call on my life to preach the gospel.

As my dad likes to say, "A call to preach is a call to prepare." So a little more than a year after sitting at Craig's funeral, we loaded up the family minivan and headed north to drop me off at Bible college. Little did I know it then, but the hurt I would endure from white evangelicalism at my school would mark me for life.

Much has been made of the legalism that wounds students who have attended institutions like the one I attended. Philip Yancey's *What's So Amazing About Grace?* is a good foray into this area, and I found my head moving like a bobblehead doll as he unveiled his Bible college battle scars.[13] Like the rules at Yancey's school, we weren't allowed to dance or go to the movies—though we could rent R-rated videos from Blockbuster or some other video store. Go figure. There was a dress code, and, of course, drinking, smoking, and cursing were off-limits, though there did emerge a sort of Christian cursing that became quite popular on campus, with words like *freaking* and *oh stink* to replace . . . well, you understand.

One of the things I immediately felt at my Bible college was that people of color did not seem to matter in white evangelicalism. When my wife and I first got married, I remember a few heated conversations that had the same common denominator. I would be preaching somewhere and afterwards shake hands with the people of the congregation. Inevitably a woman would come up to speak to me, and with my wife standing at my side, I wouldn't think to introduce her. There was no getting around it—Korie just wasn't on my mind, and this act of forgetfulness would inspire one of those marital realignment sessions, where the essence of her argument was that *she matters.* It didn't matter how much I tried to tell her she did, the fact that I didn't make mention of her communicated a devastating message: *You don't really matter.* My actions betrayed the truth.

My experience in Bible college reminds me of the book *The Invisible Man,* written by Ralph Ellison. The protagonist has no name. This is a masterful move on Ellison's part, because what he wants to show is the inhumanity of anonymity. When your name is never called—when you are never addressed by that name—you are being told you don't really matter. In far too many of our Christian colleges, universities, and seminaries, people of color are just like Ralph Ellison's protagonist: *nameless.*

When people of color are left off the required reading lists of the syllabi, not referred to in class discussions, not pursued for significant faculty and staff positions, or represent a small percentage of chapel speakers, white evangelicalism sends the clear message that we don't matter.

Now this may not be congruent with its heart, but if I wanted to know what you were passionate about, I would just need a few interactions to hear you speak and I'd be able to tell you. As Jesus said, "The mouth speaks what the heart is full of" (Luke 6:45). When people of color are not mentioned in substantive ways in white spaces, we're just not on your heart, and if we're not on your heart, you are telling us we don't really matter.

CHAPTER 6

Crash Course

I lost my theological virginity in the fall of 1991. Donned in baggy pants and a Cross Colours shirt, along with the appropriate aerodynamic haircut, I finally began the process of preparing for a life of preaching and teaching in what I thought was a spiritual utopia where everyone loved Jesus, and I for sure would not have to deal with issues of race. Oh how naive I was! Not long into my studies, the professors began to introduce me to something called "dispensationalism." At the time, I thought nothing of the fact that each of my theology classes required not just any old Bible, but a Bible with special commentary by a man named C. I. Scofield—one of the chief peddlers of dispensational theology. We were also given a text written by another gatekeeper (Dr. Charles Ryrie) of this brand of theology, *Dispensationalism Today*.[14]

My wife will tell you I'm the worst when it comes to remembering time and specific events as they happened, along with things like what exactly was said—although she doesn't hesitate to point out the irony of me being able to memorize a sermon yet forget what she asked me to pick up on the way home from work. So you'll have to understand if I speak broadly when it comes to what my professors communicated to me more than a quarter-century ago.

I had never heard the word *dispensationalism* before, which was odd because I was no novice to church or theology. My pastor growing up was a thoroughly biblical preacher, though I did find some of his conclusions odd—like the time he said there were certain things a married woman shouldn't wear in the bedroom. I don't know how old I was when I heard it, but I do remember bringing the subject up over lunch and my mother looking at my father and my father telling me to wait until I was thirteen to discuss this further.

My pastor was more of what we would call a biblical theologian, and what I was being introduced to in the halls of my Bible college was something I had never heard of before: *systematic theology*. This kind of theology is extraordinarily helpful when we approach the Scriptures in that it helps us, like a basketball player, to palm our Bibles. You know, to find our bearings and understand what's happening in the epochs of biblical history. A dispensational approach keeps me from biblical vertigo as I try to make sense of the law and how it applies to my life today, if at all.

But the problem with any systematic approach to God is that we can't contain the Infinite in any finite, man-made structure. Like trying to close a trunk stuffed with too many clothes, parts of God will always ooze out of one's little biblical box. No matter what your system is, there will always be, "But what about *that* verse?" Given this, we'd all be wise to take Kendrick Lamar's advice when it comes to our cute little systems and just be "Humble."

But this was not how dispensationalism was taught to me. Imagine my distress when I came across a line in Ryrie's *Dispensationalism Today* declaring that the sine qua non of dispensationalism is a literal herme-neutic.[15] This floored me.

Maybe I should back up a bit. In case you're wondering what dispensationalism is, you should know the professors who introduced me to it in the early 1990s had in mind a specific brand of dispensationalism called classic, or traditional, dispensationalism, not to be confused with what we would now call progressive dispensationalism. To keep things simple, classic dispensationalism sees Israel and the church as two separate entities that have no real points of continuity. What's more, classic dispensationalism says the kingdom is yet future, and therefore to the classic dispensationalist, the focus should be on the soul and not really on the body and on issues of justice.

Forgive me if I'm being a bit blunt or crass with my theological definitions, but this is how it was unveiled to us. I can't tell you how many times I'd drift off during a lecture or set Ryrie's book down after reading a passage and think of the implications of a theology that only thought of the kingdom in futuristic terms. My cowardice would not let me ask these lettered professors if dispensationalists marched in the streets with Dr. King during the struggle for civil rights. I knew the answer to that one—they were off at some prophecy conference guesstimating the day of the return of Jesus Christ.

CHAPTER 7

Like Robin Hood

D ispensationalism is a theology crafted by white, middle-class hands. I'm not being unduly harsh here, because, again, it is impossible to do theology totally divested of one's ethnic lenses and outlook. As a black man, it is impossible for me to read of the jealousy that Daniel's Gentile coworkers felt at the news of his impending promotion and not feel the impulse to cry racism and file some sort of an HR complaint (see Daniel 6). There will always be those portions of Scripture that my blackness will flinch at. We all bring our ethnic crayons to the text. It just is what it is.

I'm worried that using this illustration of dispensationalism may lose you. So maybe it's helpful to jump ahead a few years before we double back and tidy some things up. Dispensationalism is more like a pair of Jordache jeans in the retail store of theology—out of fashion. The "in" look today is Calvinism, or Reformed theology–which is like a vintage car that only gets more and more popular over time. As a matter of full disclosure, you should know that I consider myself reformed . . . with a lowercase "r." However, let's remember, it too is a system and as such should be held humbly. Hebrews 6 and 10, along with a host of other naughty passages, have been driving *Reformed* people nuts for years. Again, Kendrick Lamar proves helpful: be "Humble."

As a black man, I still find myself getting an allergic reaction from time to time to Reformed theology. At the epicenter of this systematic approach is the sovereignty of God. I *do* believe in the sovereignty of God; however, it's easy to buy into this system, popularized by a white man (John Calvin), when you belong to a race of people who have been on the historic "right side" of sovereignty. But when you've been sailed through the Middle Passage, packed in under inhumane conditions, inspected and sold on auction blocks, separated from your parents or loved ones, and forced to engage in sexually immoral acts for breeding purposes, you can see how my esophagus might tighten over certain dimensions of Reformed theology. Yes, black people (including me) have bought in to this brand of theology going back centuries, but that doesn't negate the reality that it is a theology primarily done in white.

Back to dispensationalism. In order to sell dispensationalism (including its younger brother, "progressive dispensationalism," which sees the kingdom as both now and future, as opposed to classic dispensationalism, which has only seen the future dimensions of the kingdom), its peddlers say it is the result of a "literal hermeneutic." Talk about a sleight of hand. What is meant by this phrase is that if one would just read their Bible plainly, *the natural conclusion is dispensationalism, silly. I mean, come on, everybody knows this, don't they?* Here is where white evangelicalism becomes pernicious.

I thought back to the hundreds of sermons I heard from my black pastor, Dr. Herman Conley. What married women wore in the bedroom aside, he gave us a steady diet of the Word of God. So why had I never heard of dispensationalism until I left the black church and came to my almost all-white school in the north? Why is it today that if you walk into the vast majority of urban churches and say the word *dispensationalism*, they would (at best) look at you as if you had just spoken in tongues? Why hadn't we done prophecy conferences outfitted with the requisite flannel board timelines and flip charts? I had no other recourse but to conclude that my black church in Atlanta had been guilty of bad theology. The white man had opened my eyes. Like it was for Robin Hood, it was time for me to "steal" this biblical theology and take it back to my poor black friends who had been deprived for so long.

CHAPTER 8

"Saving" the Black Church

There is an evil I have seen under the sun: the minority descendants of schools steeped in white evangelicalism often graduate with a deep disenchantment with their churches of origin. It's the student who was raised in the urban church who now returns home on break or postgraduation determined to give his congregation an unsolicited theological "wheel alignment." It is as if they have experienced a type of pseudo-"wokeness" compelling them to critique and at times even condemn the very churches God used to lay the foundation for their faith.

At issue here, again, is not white evangelicals or even their theological offerings. Rather it is when those offerings are presented as the result of some "literal hermeneutic" and normalized as the plumb line to measure our preaching and practice. Many people of color then take these plumb lines and hold them up to their churches and pastors, assuming any lack of theological compliance to the plumb line of white evangelicalism thereby equals heretical preaching and a faulty philosophy of ministry. Many end up so frustrated with their black, Chinese, or Hispanic church (to name just a few) that they file for divorce and look for their next bride—white evangelicalism—but rarely does the second wife fully satisfy.

I never divorced the black church, but we did file for separation. Only months after my graduation from Bible college, I found myself immersed in the ordination process initiated by my home church.

They were so proud of me and my accomplishments, and they were ready to embrace me as a returning son. That excitement would quickly dissipate.

As is often the case with young people, I allowed my idealism to run amok. Seated before the ordination council, bracing for my oral examination, I seized the opportunity to put them in their doctrinal place. My answers were punchy. My attitude was terse and taut. There was no humility as I gave them smug, "left-handed" responses laced with unbiblical sarcasm. Many of my answers began with, "Of course as we all know," knowing full well they didn't know. These well-meaning and hardworking men learned about dispensationalism and asked me to repeat for them what I meant by *premillennialism* (the view that the second coming of Christ will occur before the thousand-year reign of Christ, also known as the millennium). They responded to my brashness with grace and humility. A few of them could have been my grandfather, all of them my father. I thank God that my father was not in the room, for he would have grabbed me by my proverbial ear and given me the kind of good tongue lashing a petulant two-year-old deserved, even though at the time I was twenty-two.

My salvific posture was fueled by many conversations I held with my minority classmates in the halls of white evangelicalism. We dreamed of going back to the black church to save her. Long after class had ended, we huddled around a table tucked away in a corner of the student center and talked about all the problems with our churches as if they were unique to our churches. In our collective naïveté, we thought it was the urban church that had a monopoly on bad theology, unaccountable leaders, thin preaching, and ill-formed disciples. What's more, the diagnosis we had rendered was grossly overstated. In response to reports that he was on his deathbed, Mark Twain wrote a letter that read, "The report of my death was an exaggeration"—and reports of urban churches' demise have likewise been greatly exaggerated. Minority churches are no worse off than white ones. But white evangelicalism would have us think otherwise.

I want to be fair here. Not once did my professors in Bible college or seminary say anything disparaging about our churches. I don't even recall being remotely prompted by them to go back and be a part of the "solution." But this is what makes white evangelicalism dangerous. When you take the posture of a learner and all of your disciplers are white, a power dynamic exists that is bound to have its share of casualties.

Discipleship in any arena presupposes a power dynamic. I know that in a postmodern society such as ours, terms like *power* can be upsetting, but I do not use the word in any sort of pejorative sense. To make a disciple presupposes that the one making the disciple is more of a representative of the ideal than the one being formed. When Paul lays his cards on the table to the Colossians and tells them he exists to present people mature in Christ (Colossians 1:28), he is assuming (1) they are immature; (2) he is more mature; and (3) he has the requisite resources to aid and assist them in their journey to Christlike maturity. These are the simple facts of discipleship.

There is no real coercion in true discipleship. What lures the person being discipled is the degree to which they are impressed with the person who is discipling them. There exists that sense of "I want what you have." Why would the disciples leave their homes to follow Jesus? Why would a young Timothy wave good-bye to his mother and grandmother and set off with Paul? I felt this with the tribe of men who have discipled me over the years. Why else would I spend money to accompany them on mission trips or invest my most valuable resource of time?

A major segment of one's spiritual formation and discipleship is *education*, be it formal or informal. If one uses the paradigm of head, hands, and heart to erect a scaffolding of discipleship, then we see the role that Bible colleges and seminaries play in making disciples. In Christian higher education, the ones who are invested with the power dynamic to discipleship are the professors. Now this may not have been stated on the job description when they signed on, but it is a part of the terrain. When a professor walks into the classroom and embarks on a

New Testament Survey journey as students type furiously on their computers, he is functioning as a proverbial Paul. There's no escaping this.

What doesn't get talked about enough in discipleship is the residue. In any disciple-making encounter, one leaves fingerprints marked with their own sort of DNA, and a part of that DNA is informed by their ethnicity and culture. Discipleship demands the transference of one's life. Run as one may from this, who you are is bound to ooze out to some degree.

Jesus understood this. In one of his redemptively ornery moments, Jesus chastised the Pharisees about how they went about making disciples: "Woe to you, teachers of the law and Pharisees, you hypocrites! You travel over land and sea to win a single convert, and when you have succeeded, you make them twice as much a child of hell as you are" (Matthew 23:15).

Now let's not be too hard on the Pharisees. I don't think they intended to produce "a child of hell." They had every intention to transfer to their mentees their love for and understanding of God's Word. What they didn't realize was that disciple making always involves more than what you're saying. Remember, Jesus critiqued them for being lovers of money, along with other faulty character traits. All of this—love for God's Word, strict adherence to it, love for money, cultural norms, and more—they passed on to their spiritual children through the umbilical cord of discipleship. Though some may see it as trite, it's true that discipleship is more caught than taught.

In my day, I saw many black men enter my Bible college adorned in Malcolm X hats with Public Enemy–inspired African medallions dangling from their necks, only to prefer khaki pants and button-down shirts four years later. The results have been devastating. Some so learned to hate their churches of origin that they filed for divorce, never to return. Others came back as messiahs of some sort, only to experience John 1:11 in real time: "He came to that which was his own, but his own did not receive him."

There's a naughty little secret that some of us minorities are in on when it comes to disciple making and white evangelicalism. I have seen people of color who have been discipled solely by our white siblings, who in turn subconsciously try to outwhite their white disciplers. Part of this is due to our upbringing, where we were told that in order to do well, we had to work twice as hard as our white peers to procure advancement. This, I'm convinced, plagues the subconscious of people of color and carries over into the discipleship moment, where we take not only the message but even the cultural trappings it came packaged in and seek to outdo those who have discipled us. It's hard to hold well-meaning white evangelicals culpable for this tragedy, because the power dynamic is multiplied exponentially when discipleship happens cross-ethnically from the representative of historic power and oppression in our nation to the recipient of that historic oppression.

Mix into this the impulse of white idolization that runs so rampant among children of the diaspora (people originally from one country who have now been scattered, or dispersed, across another country, such as America) adrift in the streams of white evangelicalism, and you have a toxic chemical threatening to eat away at the very identity pillars of the one being formed. I cannot tell you how many times I've been sneezed on by minorities due to some allergic reaction they've had to their ethnic churches of origin. So they accuse me of not being Reformed enough, for example. After a little probing on my part, I discover they just finished their first Puritan book or had been binge-watching the latest white preacher who is more Calvin than Calvin. We need to do better.

But what is better? There are two sides to the table here. On my side, minorities need to be careful to include other minorities in their spiritual formation journey. You need Jesus-loving people who look like you to help form you more into the image of God. As Will Smith said in the movie *Hitch*, "'You' is a very fluid concept."

Too much of discipleship is gnostic in its philosophy, choosing to address only matters of the spirit and not the body. But when one understands that God created my flesh—my literal body—and that the theology of incarnation means God came in the flesh, then any adequate discipleship strategy must address all of the dimensions of my life, including concepts connected to my body such as race (if you think race should be ignored, it won't be in heaven; see Revelation 5 and 7). Therefore, we need to include people who look like us to disciple us.

I know of far too many minorities who haven't experienced this. Like the black rocker-turned-country singer Darius Rucker, there are far too many Christ-following people of color who are brilliant and gifted—and tragically marginalized. Their own won't hear them, because they are perceived as having turned their backs on them. There's nothing wrong with playing a little country from time to time, but we need more minorities to play notes that touch the heartstrings of their fellow countrymen as well. It is because of this that I feel a profound responsibility to say yes to as many young black men as possible who ask me to mentor them.

On the other side of the table, I'm not saying that whites should not disciple minorities. Jesus reminds us the Great Commission is multiethnic and involves cross-ethnic and cultural encounters: "Therefore go and make disciples of all nations" (Matthew 28:19). However, when one fails to see the totality of what they are transferring in the journey of fulfilling the Great Commission, they do violence to Jesus' command and to the individual.

It's somewhat like the white parent of the black adopted child who refuses to learn how to properly do their hair or to introduce them to their ethnic kin. The white professor who opens his Bible to impart to his eager diverse students must own and articulate—like all of us—his ethnic limitations. The disciplers, no matter their ethnicity, must seek opportune moments to posture themselves as learners, gleaning from the rich cultural experiences and tragic hurts of the ethnic others seated across the table from them. This is easily done by asking questions, entering into the disciples' world by attending their churches, and inquiring about formative writings written by people of color in order to glean from them.

It's sad to look back on my graduation day and realize that the four years steeped in white evangelicalism actually placed me at a disadvantage when compared to my white classmates. While we were both learning deep truths from the Scriptures, they were at the same time having their ethnic identity and worldview affirmed, while mine were being completely denied and diminished. It would take me years to make up the difference.

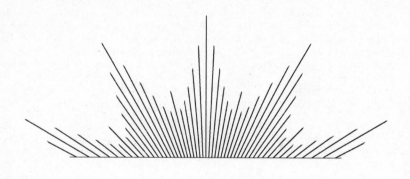

Minority
Owned

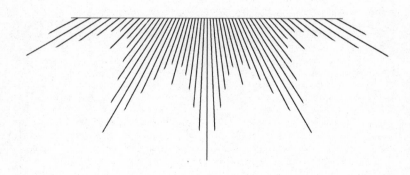

CHAPTER 9

The Real Problem
of Privilege

I've been asked by young leaders to tell them how I "arrived" to where I am in ministry today. Their question is an embarrassing one, filled with silent hopes for some grand recipe—that if they follow the same well-thought-out instructions, they'll also "arrive" one day. But I quickly disappoint them. No such recipe exists. Peering through the rearview mirror of my journey is laughable. I'm just not that smart. Nor am I so arrogant as to think that God is using me in the way he is because of some grand strategic plan that I'm implementing to a T—where all I have to do is work hard and pull myself up by my Timberlands. It didn't take me long to figure out that whatever plans I may concoct should be etched in pencil. God is orchestrating everything.

I often bristle at the phrase *white privilege*. It's so harsh and unfair. Just about all of us have a portion of privilege heaped on our plates. While my ethnicity does place me at a disadvantage in many arenas, the fact that my parents are still married and deeply love Jesus and that my father is well respected and actively engaged in my life is a measure of privilege whose aftershocks I continue to feel. Privilege is never the problem; *it's the stewardship of privilege that's the issue*. Just ask Jesus. No one came into this world more "privileged" than Jesus—the one and only Son of God. I'm grateful he leveraged his privilege for my good.

As a child of privilege and a recent college graduate, I found that my father's name opened doors for me immediately. I wince at these words, but there's no getting around it. While my former classmates were scrambling for jobs, the last name Loritts got me accepted into a summer internship with one of the nation's premier pastors, Dr. Tony Evans, along with unprecedented access to him during the weeks following my graduation.

Looking back on my time with him in the summer of 1995, I remember waging one-on-one basketball battles in his driveway (he is competitive!), having late-night theological discussions, and gleaning pearls of preaching wisdom, where he'd often say, "Loritts, you must learn to think illustratively." To help me with this, he would demand that I (along with the other interns) provide him with at least twenty-five illustrations a week. I would swell up with pride on the rare occasion he used one on a Sunday. I am who I am today because of his influence.

One particular Sunday during my time with Dr. Evans remains tattooed across my mind. Wrapping up his sermon, he invited everyone in the church who was on welfare to come down front. I remember thinking, *This ought to be interesting,* and then, *I think I'd rather walk down the aisle to confess shacking up with another woman than admit to this.* But sure enough, the altar was flooded with people. Then Dr. Evans pronounced that he was going to provide a tangible fix to their situation. In the weeks to come, a computer lab was set up for all who had come to the altar, and a partnership was formed with an affluent church on the other side of town, where several of their members owned businesses and had promised jobs to those who were trained in computer literacy at the church Dr. Evans pastored. Months later, scores of people waved good-bye to welfare and had been given the dignity of work.

My head was spinning. Sure, I had grown up in the black church and had seen us muddy our hands in issues of poverty and injustice, but I had never witnessed something like this emerge from a graduate of a school steeped in white evangelicalism. It was the first time I had seen a person who looked like me and who had graduated from a school like the one I graduated from be a champion for justice. It wouldn't be the last time.

Some months later, I was wrapping up another internship at a black church in Atlanta when I received a phone call from one of my father's closest friends, Bishop Kenneth Ulmer—who also happened to be my godfather. He said he wanted me to serve on the staff at his church. His timing couldn't have been better. I was wondering what was next. At one point, things had been really clear, but then my girlfriend and I broke up. Like most detours in life, God used a woman to reroute me. A few weeks after my godfather called, I packed my belongings into my burgundy Nissan Sentra on a cold December day and ventured out onto I-20 with a broken yet hopeful heart, headed for Inglewood, California.

My godfather defies labels. He is the Ray Charles of pastoral ministry. He grew up as a musical prodigy in East St. Louis. "Little Kenny Ulmer" was so good that he played for Mahalia Jackson at a young age and was asked to travel and play with the "King of Gospel"—James Cleveland (he turned down the offer). In the late sixties, Bishop Ulmer landed in California, where he ended up becoming the organist at one of the marquee black churches in Los Angeles, pastored by Dr. Melvin Wade. Seated at the organ one Sunday, my godfather says he received the call to ministry. Newly married, he, like my dad, concluded that a call to preach is a call to prepare. So he enrolled in a school steeped in white evangelicalism, earning a Master of Theology and then a PhD. Not long into his studies, he was called to be the third pastor of the Faithful Central Missionary Baptist Church, located at the time on 61st and Hoover in the heart of South Central Los Angeles.

Faithful Central was bursting at the seams when I landed there in the winter of 1995. They were packing out a warehouse that seated about a thousand people—four times on Sundays—and I had a bird's-eye view of it all. My job was to simply stay close and do whatever Bishop asked me to do in this all-black church.

I did everything. I preached and washed his car. I picked up his clothes from the cleaners. I picked up world-famous pastors he had booked to preach at our church from the Los Angeles airport. I eaves-dropped on intense conversations he had with legendary black pastors and leaders like Dr. E. V. Hill as I sat quietly at a breakfast table on Crenshaw Boulevard. I was his chauffer, escorting him around town as he preached at anniversary celebrations for huge and small black churches alike. I would literally lie on the floor of his home study, littered with thousands of books ranging from authors like John MacArthur to E. K. Bailey, just watching him prepare. Kenneth Carver Ulmer represented the possibilities of what I could become.

If you know anything about the black church, it has what is called a "rostrum of ministers." This is where a discipleship of sorts happens for my people. Sometimes things can become a bit chippy as young ministers jockey for position to gain favor with the pastor so they can have more time in the pulpit. I never had to do this. Bishop Ulmer showed me unusual kindness, having me sit next to him on the platform at all four services, which I was happy to attend. Sunday mornings at Faithful Central were magical. I would watch him get up and direct the choir or slide over to the organ, working the crowd into a frenzy, while moments later he was exegeting the Greek as he walked us through a multi-year study of the book of 1 Corinthians.

Bishop Ulmer is a paradox—an unparalleled exegete who spoke in tongues, a whooping preacher with a PhD from a white evangelical school, and the possessor of a preaching gift so large that he preaches for both exuberant Pentecostal churches and audibly subdued conservative churches. He's sort of like the apostle Paul, who could be found in the synagogue one moment and up on Mars Hill "in revival" the next. Spellbound, I often thought to myself while watching Bishop preach, *I want a gift big enough to preach at First African Methodist Episcopal and First Presbyterian.*

You can see why, not long after landing at Faithful Central, I exhaled and told myself this was home and I'd never leave. I had to learn the hard way that God loves it when you tell him what you will and won't do.

CHAPTER 10

Searching for Home

In the movie *Antwone Fisher*, we meet a young twentysomething black man who has no real sense of identity or belonging. His father had been murdered, and his mother was nowhere to be found. His childhood set him adrift from foster home to foster home where he experienced the ugliness of unwantedness and abuse. One of his foster moms so despised him that she rarely called him by his given name, choosing instead to refer to him as "nigger."

After a bit of prodding by his therapist, he decides to find his mother. Successful, he returns from his emotional reunion with her, back to a house surprisingly packed with distant relatives. Overwhelmed by all the introductions to kin he never knew existed, he sees the dining room door slowly open and there is the matriarch of the family overlooking a table crowded with food. Stretching her withered hands toward him, she welcomes him. Antwone is finally home.

This was an everyday experience for me during my years at Faithful Central. The sounds emanating from the organist as he underscored Bishop's climactic closing touched a place in me that had been buried beneath theology texts and lectures the previous four years in Bible college. The banter with my ethnic kin reminded me that I was home. The fact that I no longer needed to interpret some racial insider talk or decode anything like I had spent the previous four years doing caused me to breathe a sigh of relief. I was home, and I never wanted to leave.

My three years at Faithful Central dismissed any messianic inclinations I maintained that the black church needed saving. Hearing Bishop Ulmer wear out the Greek syntax of a Pauline epistle and then scream, "Early Sunday," at the close heaped hot coals of shame on my head over my theological arrogance. Seeing Faithful Central feed the poor and provide free HIV/AIDS blood tests and counseling in the midst of the epidemic of the 1990s showed me it was possible to have a ministry philosophy that carried the twins of orthodoxy and orthopraxy in the womb of the local church. I was home.

There were rare moments when I felt like I was more an animal at a zoo being observed than a lost son having returned home though. Given the popularity of our church, we became a tourist stop for white evangelicals during spring and summer breaks. Impossible to ignore, these large white groups would file in with matching T-shirts and sit in the same row, rocking to the music and genuinely enjoying the sermon. Afterward they were far too predictable, commenting on how long they had sat in church, saying it as if they needed to be commended for such a sacrifice. Sometimes the conversations turned awkward, like the time one man asked to be taken to the nearest crack house. Even his colleagues picked up on his misstep and seemed embarrassed by his condescension. Like antebellum servants who had heard their masters disparage black people, only to return the favor moments later out of earshot, once this group filed out, we were instructed to drop him off at the local crack house and leave him there for a prolonged period of time. We howled as we waved good-bye to him.

These historically long Sunday services our white friends endured usually came at the tail end of a week they had spent helping us. We were their mission field, where they tutored our kids, built or renovated our homes, or helped with vacation Bible school. This sort of thing continues to go on, and while I'm grateful for it, I'm not sure how appropriate it is in the long run.

Far too many white evangelicals solely have relationships with minorities whom they help. If all of our relationships with a group of people are from a helping posture, one is bound to entrench the very thing we're hopefully trying to dismantle—namely, inequality. White folks need peer relationships with people of color *who don't just need them*. People like me. I have good credit, and I can take you out to lunch and pay for it. I own my own home, and I don't need your help. But as long as the only people of color our white siblings engage with are minority orphans on a mission trip who pose for a picture with them that gets posted on social media pages, the problems will continue to plague us well after I'm gone.

CHAPTER 11

Birthed Out of Rejection

O n a Sunday in the late 1700s, a black man walked into a church and began praying. What he didn't realize was that he was doing so in the whites-only section of the church. Incensed by his audacity, the people around him immediately confronted him and tossed him outside onto the streets of Philadelphia. African Americans were so appalled by what they had witnessed that they left the church and formed what would become the African Methodist Episcopal Church.

This bit of a history lesson is not to incite guilt, for we are a resilient people, and one of the most mystifying truths is how we have held on to something that rejected us and was used as justification to enslave the likes of my great-great-grandfather, who was led to faith by his enslavers. As the songwriter was wont to say, "God moves in a mysterious way." The black church was birthed out of rejection. Just about every historic black denomination is the offspring of white folks wanting nothing to do with us.

The real tragedy is not what happened back in the 1700s, but that the black church continues to endure rejection in the twenty-first century. Sure, I've seen our white siblings visit the African-American churches I've served and genuinely enjoy all of the elements of the experience. But there is a difference between visiting and joining, between being a guest and locking arms in covenant partnership.

Now granted, I've never looked for white people to join our church in Inglewood or in Dr. Evans's church in Dallas. But I often wondered why whites would not come to these churches. Sure, Faithful Central is in Inglewood, but if you know anything about Los Angeles, there are white enclaves tucked away not far from the church. When I worked for Bishop Ulmer, I didn't hear one "sort of okay" sermon. They were all home runs—like, "leave you speechless for fifty minutes" home runs. And I heard the same one four times a Sunday and never—and I mean never—grew tired of it. Bishop had everything a person could ask for in a preacher—depth, educational credentials, heartfelt applications, charisma, humor, you name it. But still, white evangelicals never joined us. You can't tell me that if he shared melanin with them, things wouldn't be different.

It's funny how the tables turn with age. Like an adult child helping to raise her aging parents, I find myself giving advice to my aging mentor and godfather. With the NFL coming to Inglewood (both the Rams and the Chargers will begin playing there in 2020), Bishop Ulmer says, "White folks are coming here three on a mule."

Gentrification is not only changing neighborhoods, but it is also threatening to unravel the core fabric of minority communities—ethnically indigenous churches. For those who live in but don't own in these gentrifying neighborhoods, it won't be long until their paychecks will no longer be able to keep pace with their rising rents. And for longtime home owners, the allure of cashing out and moving to a much more affordable community is too appealing to not join in the exodus.

Okay, so white folks never wanted us. I get that. Not only have we made things work; we actually kind of—forgive me for saying it—enjoyed the separation because it gave us a sense of autonomy and power and a safe haven for our unique cultural expression without having to accommodate or put up a front. But white evangelicalism does not have the right to throw us out on the street and then judge our theology or scoff at our decisions. How arrogant of white evangelicalism to get rid of us and then critique our "poor theology"! That's like me divorcing my wife, refusing to make child support payments, and ridiculing her for the decrepit condition of her new home.

I once had a conversation with an elderly African-American man who had served for years as a bivocational pastor. During his tenure, he found himself so hungry to learn more of God's Word that he petitioned a well-known conservative seminary to let him take courses. They refused. He then asked if it was okay for him to audit a theology class. After much discussion they finally acquiesced on the condition that he sit outside the classroom. He said there were times he sat in the rain just to learn the Scriptures at this all-white institution. No other African Americans would join him in sitting outside. They either went to other schools that would accept them or were self-taught.

While it's ill-informed to levy the verdict of poor theology on minority churches, let's suppose that white evangelicalism is completely right (she's not though). Who, then, is to blame for this current state of affairs? Which seminaries have reached out to people of color to welcome us into their schools to learn?

I'll answer it this way: In April 1961, Martin Luther King Jr. preached at Southern Seminary. How could a Southern Baptist institution invite a black man aiming to take down racial injustice to preach at their school? Well, they were liberal then. Oh, yeah, that's right. By and large, it was liberal institutions that welcomed us without making us stoop to the indignity of inhumanity. White evangelicalism wants to have its proverbial cake and eat it too—critiquing our historical "bad theology" and yet not accepting ownership for refusing to educate us in ways that validated our biblical anthropology as fellow creatures made in the *imago Dei*.

The way white evangelicalism works around this is to construct a theology that allows them to wriggle out of personal responsibility for historical injustices. In their seminal work titled *Divided by Faith*, Michael Emerson and Christian Smith point out how white evangelicalism dismisses structural injustice and therefore its own complicit personal culpability.[16] The problem is that the Bible paints another picture.

When Jesus encounters Zacchaeus, we are told he is not only a tax collector, whose bank account is replenished daily by greedy injustice, but he is a "chief tax collector" (Luke 19:2). This means that Zacchaeus is an architect of systemic injustice, predicated on a network of fraudulent tax collectors who scheme against and extort people for their salacious endeavors. He is the head of the Jericho cartel. Jesus invites himself over to this man's house, and the train wreck of the gospel invades his soul. It's here that Zacchaeus confesses, "Look, Lord! Here and now I give half of my possessions to the poor, and if I have cheated anybody out of anything, I will pay back four times the amount" (Luke 19:8). The good news—namely, salvation—has made him acutely aware of and deeply convicted about his participation in systemic injustice. Jesus responds, "Today salvation has come to this house" (verse 9).

A lot has been made in recent years about the term *gospel*. Books have been written about the need to be "gospel-centered," to live "The Explicit Gospel," along with events inviting us to come "Together for the Gospel." Now these resources and events are extremely needed and nourishing, yet for all of our gospel talk, little has been made over a subset of the gospel known as *restitution*. Note that I didn't say *reparations*. Reparations are governmentally legislated, and I'm not attaching any sort of moral equivalency to the term. Gospel restitution is the Spirit-induced response to any vestiges of culpability when it comes to matters of injustice. But notice that gospel restitution is not just a feeling, but it involves a tangible giving back as a necessary act of repentance. When Zacchaeus offers to tangibly restore in material ways the ones he has both defrauded and impoverished, Jesus affirms his salvation.

I have white friends who are direct descendants of ancestors who are on record for defrauding and building businesses on unjust systems (like Jim Crow), and these friends wrestle deeply with this. One of them has confessed he must own his ancestors' injustices and right the wrongs. So he does it in remarkable ways by taking a significant portion of his wealth and investing it in homes for the poor. What would Jesus say to this? "Today salvation has come to your home."

But because white evangelicalism has constructed a personal Jesus who (at best) winks at systemic injustice and pats the victims on the back, saying with a sigh, "That's too bad; pull yourself up like the rest of us and keep moving," she never autocorrects the injustice and is therefore doomed to commit more wrong. This sort of thing continues today as the kissing cousins of gentrification and church planting have landed back in the cities, transforming ghettos into whites-only neighborhoods. You do see how this becomes problematic for historically urban churches, don't you?

I recently was invited by a group of Oakland pastors to talk to them about racial reconciliation. The group was made up of all African Americans, and as they shared, it felt as if we were at a funeral, eulogizing the Oakland of the latter part of the twentieth century. Gentrification is sweeping through the city at a sprinter's stride. What were once large minority churches have now been decimated, as their constituency is moving further east in search of affordable housing. "If we don't figure out a way to get white people in the doors, we are dead," one pastor exhaled, expressing the exact sentiments of my godfather. But with new church planters moving in to engage the new demographic, these black pastors could see the writing on the wall. They had as much of a chance of whites joining their churches as someone hitting the jackpot in the lottery.

White evangelicalism can do something about this. In what would be a historically unprecedented move, our white siblings can choose to follow minority leadership, serve in minority churches, and learn from minority preaching. This is what Reggie Williams points out in his book *Bonhoeffer's Black Jesus*.[17] At the height of the Harlem Renaissance, the German theologian Dietrich Bonhoeffer chose to join the Abyssinian Baptist Church in Harlem—a large black church. Bonhoeffer's life was enriched, for it was here that he heard the gospel in all of its glorious dimensions, compelling him to go back and stand up for oppressed Jews in Europe. Had he done what most whites who have just landed in some new city now do—join a church plant or find an existing church that looks like them—it is doubtful we would have ever heard of Bonhoeffer and his exploits. Praise God that he chose a different path, one that allowed him to follow ethnically indigenous leaders.

The modern church-planting movement is oftentimes a silent partner in systemic injustice, refusing to demand that its leaders consider simply learning from existing churches in these gentrifying neighborhoods. So they set up shop and take aim at their target demographic— white urban hipsters. This becomes a sort of spiritual colonization. Never once does it cross their minds that there are already some good churches there, and they might be able to help support, strengthen, and revitalize existing ministries, not by taking over and leading, but by showing up and learning.

White evangelicals have played an essential role in my growth and development. Shoot, some of my best friends are white evangelicals! Seriously. But white evangelicalism as a predominant exclusive system is a whole different thing. The latter (white evangelicalism) must die, for it never teaches its subscribers an ethnic proactivity birthed out of a gospel humility, willing to bend itself in submission to leaders already engaged in kingdom work who may not look like them.

CHAPTER 12

Whose Table Is It?

Because I felt at home in the black church, I also felt something I hadn't felt in a long time—safe. My years spent in white evangelicalism left me feeling like a black man going to visit his white girlfriend's family in Memphis for the first time. There was a pervasive sense that I was being acutely watched, followed even. Every word as a guest in white evangelicalism had to be measured. I didn't quite understand what my father meant after I told him I was leaving Faithful Central to work full-time at a white church across town that had never had a black pastor in their one hundred plus years of existence. But as we hung up the phone, he pleaded with me, "Be careful."

In some sense, I didn't so much choose to leave Faithful Central as I was called and compelled by God to exit. The few short months marking the spring of 1998 would prove to be the most dramatic of my life. God seemed to move at a sprinter's pace during that window of time, orchestrating events as if some kind of deadline was closing in on him.

Of course, a girl was involved. It was a January day when I first laid eyes on the woman who would become my wife. I was seated on the stage one Sunday in worship, and the lights seemed to envelop this lone woman in a sea of thousands. I forgot the words to the song. Entranced and staring, I lost all sense of propriety and decorum. The pastor next to me on the platform asked me in hushed tones what was wrong. I pointed out the woman, whom the lighting girl had clearly singled out, and told him this was the most beautiful woman I had ever seen. He shook his head, told me she was out of my league, and that if for some random reason she were to ever agree to a date with me, he'd pay for it. In case you're wondering what pastors talk about in church, it's not always some deep theological truth.

After a bit of strategizing, she agreed to go out with me, and we fell in love quickly—me the black man with pastoral ambitions, and her the half-white, half-Mexican (but *all* fine) woman who had just become a follower of Jesus. Granted, I'd never told myself I would marry a black woman; I just assumed it, the way people assume they'll safely make it to work when they leave home in the morning. To say I didn't see this one coming is to state the obvious, but hey, you can't help who you fall in love with. We've been together ever since that January day, and it has proven to be the second-best decision of my life.

Our romance began during my last semester at seminary. While my classmates were trying to figure out where they were going to work after graduation, I could relax, confident that I'd continue the ministry there in Inglewood among my people. Again, God loves it when you tell him what you'll do with your life. Little did I know that I was just weeks away from becoming the first African-American pastor to serve on staff at the historic Lake Avenue Church in Pasadena, California. It felt as if the earth under my feet had shifted.

Hindsight, as they say, is 20/20. God used my three-year layover at this white church as a balm to heal the pain I had harbored in my soul over the white side of my kingdom family. I hated leaving Faithful Central. I was angry—no, furious—with God for calling me away from home. It felt like I had punched my godfather in his soul when I unveiled what God was up to. He offered to more than double my salary, but this wasn't about money. In that mystical sort of way, God was calling me to leave, just like he had called me to preach. I knew it, but that didn't mean I had to like it.

I walked into Lake Avenue the way Jonah walked into Nineveh—steeled with an angry resolve to set these white people in their place.

They were people to be scolded, not friended. Like their spring break teams visiting us in the hood, I was there to help them and put them in their place.

A few weeks into my tenure, I was asked to preach by the senior pastor, Dr. Gordon Kirk, at the weekend services. This was a bit of a surprise since preaching wasn't a part of my job description, but I was grateful for the opportunity. A few weeks after he returned from vacation, Dr. Kirk invited me into his office for a chat. It was our first official sit-down since I joined the team. He said some very complimentary things about my message, and then he announced that he was doing something he had long wanted to do but hadn't had the opportunity: start a teaching team—just the two of us. I was so floored by his gesture it was as if I could hear my mother whispering in my ear, "Fix your face." I couldn't believe what I was hearing.

Gordon Kirk had graduated with a doctorate from Dallas Theological Seminary and had gone on to become an award-winning professor at Biola University. Now he was pastoring one of the most famous conservative, white evangelical churches in the country. If ever there was a poster child for white evangelicalism, it was Lake Avenue and Dr. Kirk—or so I thought. But here he was, saying he was going to divest himself to some degree of power and allow me to steward a measure of it as a twenty-five-year-old black man still practicing his burgeoning gift of preaching. I felt like Jackie Robinson sitting in Branch Rickey's office for the first time. If the pulpit is the steering wheel of the church, Dr. Kirk was going to let me get behind the wheel.

Our conversation took place some twenty years ago, and it's sad to confess that Dr. Kirk's actions that summer day still stand out. Minorities who occupy positions in staffs led by whites often find themselves with an Israelite-like frustration as they are asked to make bricks with no straw (Exodus 5:6–9). We are hired in the hopes of fostering diversity, yet deprived of the requisite power to bring about the desired change. The locus of power in the church is the pulpit, and to bar competent minorities from the sacred desk and yet still expect diversity is as silly as giving Jackie Robinson a uniform and a glove while leaving him on the bench and wondering why things haven't changed in the major leagues.

I don't know Dr. Kirk's heart, but I do know his actions. He never once said anything to me about a desire to be more diverse. As far as I can tell, I was not a part of some grand master plan to get more black folks in the doors. I may have been; who knows? All I can tell you is that he gave me the keys to the car and simply said, "I trust you." He let me preach on the gift of tongues, knowing I had come from a charismatic church and Lake Avenue at the time was anything but. He let me preach on Easter Sunday. Finally, he added to my responsibilities the Sunday evening worship service, which grew to the point where we had to add a second one. All the while, he smiled and cheered me on, even though people began to compare us. Whenever I'm tempted today to wash my hands of all white people due to some act of racism or injustice, the Holy Spirit taps me on the shoulder and brings to mind Dr. Kirk. I am who I am today because of him.

White evangelicalism has cast such a dynastic pall over the pantheon of American Christianity because of her insistence on monopolizing power. Christian higher education is predominantly led by whites, especially by those in the president's position. Not to mention the people lurking behind the scenes who make up the boards of these institutions—places where the real decision making happens. Weekly I'm inundated with phone calls by well-meaning white pastors who profess to having a heart for diversity and who want me to consult with them. Most of my trips to visit with these pastors and churches end in futility, all because they are unwilling to do the hard thing—the Dr. Gordon Kirk thing—and divest themselves of at least a modicum of power. So we stay stuck.

Any leader who is unwilling to transfer power to others has a failed view of the incarnation. Jesus Christ, who is fully God, voluntarily curtailed dimensions of his deity behind the veil of his humanity so that he might walk with and die for us. Paul gets to the heart of this in what theologians call the great "*kenosis* passage" of Philippians 2.

In a breathtaking show of humility, Jesus Christ "humbled himself by becoming obedient to death—even death on a cross!" (Philippians 2:8).

Yet what must not be lost amidst all of the theological complexities of Philippians 2 is the fact that Paul is merely using Jesus in an analogous fashion to make an ethical request. In an appeal to the church to be humble, he points to Jesus as the ultimate example of humility. If our leader refused to hoard and monopolize power, does it not follow that we must refuse to do so as well? Any leader worth their salt seeks to empower, and this only happens in a John the Baptist sort of way as we seek to become less so that others would become greater (see John 3:30).

Sociologists allude to this when they speak of "social capital." This lies at the core of J. D. Vance's epic tale *Hillbilly Elegy*.[18] Raised among poor whites dotting the Appalachian Trail, Vance would become the first in his immediate family to graduate from college. He would earn a law degree from the prestigious Yale Law School. Peering over his journey, he points out in humility the necessity of being in relationships with people who were further ahead of him and who helped him along the way by using their power to open doors to the unprecedented future he now enjoys. He wouldn't be anywhere close to where he is now if it hadn't been for those who chose to divest themselves of power and empower him within the context of relationship. Over and over again, I thought of men like Bishop Kenneth Ulmer and Gordon Kirk. Like J. D. Vance, I must confess I would not be where I am today without the generous stewardship of social capital from the likes of these men.

And yet there persists the question with regard to Jesus. Why did he leave the comforts of heaven, voluntarily veiling dimensions of his deity, choosing to empower us? It is the Christian worldview to answer simply that we were in need, having gotten ourselves in a situation devoid of any hope. The impetus for such a messianic move was *our need*.

I must tread lightly here with my analogy. Minorities are not sinners in need of white evangelicals who swoop down to save us. On the other extreme, we must acknowledge with extreme gratitude the Jesus-loving white men and women who exercised a countercultural courage by coming to the aid of people of color. Here I'm thinking of the likes of William Wilberforce and the Clapham Sect—the Church of England social reformers at the end of the eighteenth century. We are also indebted to the many Jesus-loving abolitionists who preached justice and who fought for and sheltered African-American slaves who were running for their very lives. And then there was William Carey, who changed the nature of global missions by taking on the clothing, culture, and customs of the beloved people of India, communicating deep value and dignity along the way.

However, what cannot be overlooked in any cursory survey of American Christianity, is that not only have white evangelicals monopolized power, but they have grossly misappropriated that same power, thereby placing people of color at great disadvantage. White evangelicals purchased us from auction blocks. White evangelicals owned slaves while pastoring churches. It was a white evangelical named George Whitefield who successfully lobbied for the legalization of slavery in Georgia so he could set up his plantation-funded orphanage. White evangelicals took part in stealing land from Native Americans. White evangelicals passively refused to participate in the civil rights movement. White evangelicals started their own "Christian" schools as a response to government-mandated integration. Much of the historical gaps (i.e., economic) existing in this country between whites and minorities were drilled and lengthened by white evangelicals.

If there is to be any hope for ethnic equality at the highest levels of the local church, Christian organizations, Christian higher education, and any other plots of real estate in the evangelical space, white evangelicalism must deed back to us the proverbial land we've been robbed of. This deeding back of the land can take on various forms, depending on the context. At times, it may mean divesting yourself of power and empowering the marginalized in your midst by giving qualified people meaningful roles in your church or organization. In other situations, it may mean sharing financial resources, like the Christ followers in Acts 2 did, with a view to long-term health and sustainability.

Examples abound, and yet all of these and more point to a gospel restitution in the legacy of Zacchaeus.

Lifting my finger to the wind, I feel a restlessness among people of color who occupy rooms in the Section 8 zip code of white evangelicalism. We are tired of waiting on our forty acres and a mule. There is a sincere movement of Jesus-loving children of the diaspora who loathe the posture of waiting and asking and who refuse to do so any longer. Unflinching in our commitment to the Scriptures, we feel as if it's time to own our own schools, conferences, and events. Obviously, this has already happened when one considers ethnically specific denominations such as the National Baptist Convention, USA, and others. Many of these denominations are well within the traditional categories of orthodoxy. What I'm getting at is a multiethnicity started by minorities, with tables open for whites to occupy.

No, we are *not* advocating segregation, but continually asking for what's our just due as equal members in God's family—to be considered when speaking invitations are sent out, to be on a list of presidential candidates for universities, and so forth—is exhausting. If power is not going to be shared with us within the evangelical world at the highest levels, then maybe, just maybe we need to create our own events within this space and spray paint over it the words "Minority Owned."

We are weary of being some fringe campus group. We are so over only being invited to chime in on race panels or to speak during the months of February or May at some ethnic-specific gathering where only those who are open-minded and interested come. We want more. We're tired of renting, and it's time to own. But when we own, we will be open to inviting our white family over to be a guest in our home for a change. But when they come over, they're not sitting at the head. It will be, after all, our table.

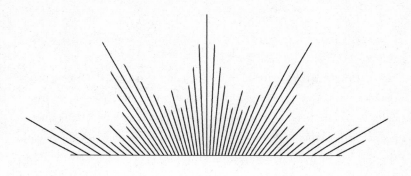

Multiethnic Sharecropping

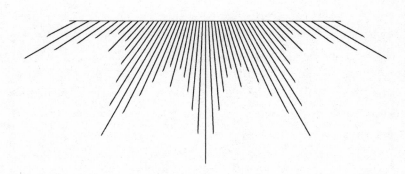

CHAPTER 13

Twelve Years in Memphis

If Memphis were a woman, she would not be pretty. Unlike her supermodel sisters of Atlanta, Charlotte, and Nashville, what attracts a person to Memphis is not the aesthetics, but the soulful grittiness of her personality. No one aspires to spend their life in Memphis unless they've grown up there or developed some sort of connection with her. In hindsight, I'm still amazed at how long I spent living there. Twelve years it was. Twelve years a Memphian.

On a cold January day, I received a phone call from a man from the hills of Kentucky whose Southern accent was so thick that had he been on television, a caption would have been needed to translate his Kentucky drawl. It was 2003, and our family was living in Charlotte, North Carolina, where I was serving a nearly all-white church as their pastor for young adults. The move from Pasadena to Charlotte felt right. California is fun, until you start a family and dream of owning a home and realize that a staff pastor's salary isn't going to quite cut it. Plus I was homesick. So when a church four hours up the road from my folks reached out, we took it, even though it was in the South.

Like my time at Lake Avenue, I found myself preaching after only a few weeks of being on staff at our new church home in Charlotte. When my sermon ended that Sunday, I was down front shaking hands when an old man sauntered up to me and some elders. Taking my hand, he turned to one of the elders and said, "We need to let this nigger preach more often." I was shocked, but not in an insulted kind of way. He used the word *nigger* like a pair of well-worn slippers—comfortable and frequent. It was just the way he talked. *What have I gotten myself into?* I thought.

Chaos is the best word to describe the twenty-two months we spent at the church in Charlotte. Massive staff transitions happened. There was anarchy on the elder board, and the pastor got caught up in a huge mess. Through it all, I was convinced that God had called us there, so I knew that when he was ready to move us, he'd do it. As my nana used to say, "He may not come when you want him, but he's always on time." Little did I know it at the time, but God came in a January phone call. When I hung up with the guy from Kentucky, I knew it may very well have been God talking to me on the other end.

It's been said that God is up to ten thousand things at any moment in our lives, but we may only be aware of a handful of them.[19] Had this man called me while in California and invited us to Memphis, there's no way Mrs. Loritts would have signed up. Shoot, that would have even been a hard sell for me. God knew this, so to soften the blow, he took us to a "new South," trendy city like Charlotte. But there was more. During this season of my life, I was receiving more and more invitations to speak at conferences and events, and when I'd get up to address the crowd, I would harbor a silent frustration over why the audiences were homogenous—either all-white or all-black. I began to dream of being a part of something multiethnic. Like Nehemiah, I ached to repair the walls. My silent frustration was being turned into a holy ambition.

A month after his phone call, my new Kentucky friend was in town with a colleague to share their hearts with our family. God had burdened them to also be a part of something multiethnic. The problem, as they saw it, was that they were two white guys whose excitement would soon be toned down by the reality of their limitations. They needed an African American on the team. "So I'm a part of your affirmative action plan," I said with a serious face that concealed my mischievousness. Finally, I laughed, and I could hear them exhale a "thank God!"

So we began to dream together. What if God wanted us to go to one of the most difficult cities in the nation—a city that had killed the leader of the civil rights movement—and plant a multiethnic church as a visible manifestation of our future eternal reality? I didn't need to hear much more. Three months later, we sold our house, lost $13,000 on the deal, and landed in Memphis, Tennessee. I had no idea what a beautiful mess the next twelve years would be!

CHAPTER 14

The Problem of the Multiethnic Church

Church planting is a lot like having a baby—an exhausting exhilaration (or so I'm told). The first few months were an adrenaline rush as we hammered out our values and scoped out places to meet. A core was beginning to gather, and word was leaking out around town about a small band of believers who wanted to start a multiethnic church. When our church launched on the first Sunday in November 2003, there was an innate sense that we were going to be a part of something big.

While our church didn't explode, it did grow steadily, like an Airbus A380 at takeoff, breaking through the clouds. A multiethnic church in Memphis was a bit of a unicorn then, so we attracted a lot of visitors. Most, if not all of our visitors, in those early days were white. We had the hardest time getting African-American Memphians to join us, and understandably so.

In the late 1800s, Memphis was on equal footing with cities like Nashville and Atlanta in terms of population. It was a tight race for who would have the title for the marquee Southern city. All of that changed when yellow fever ripped through the city in the 1870s. The worst diagnosis anyone could have received back then was yellow fever, so when whispers of it began to make their way around town, twenty-five thousand people left. Almost all of them were white, leaving fifteen thousand people behind. Once yellow fever wiped its mouth of Memphis, two thousand of the thirteen thousand were left, resulting in the city's loss of its charter. The lion's share of those two thousand were black, a legacy the city of Memphis continues to feel today.

The face of Memphis from those days forward has always been black, but the pockets of Memphis and the real power have been white. Memphis's poverty rate is among the highest in the country, with almost all of those who live below the poverty line being black. Leaving a downtown barbecue joint one evening, my then eight-year-old son saw a black man begging for food. He turned to me and said, "Dad, why are all the poor people in Memphis black?" A bit of an overstatement, but not by much. The economic disparity between whites and blacks is not just frightening, but infuriating.

Memphis has a country club that to this day prohibits blacks from joining. I've had lunch at white churches in the city where all the cooks, landscapers, and servants were black, causing me to wonder if I was at a church or a plantation. We've waited in carpool lines behind lines of fancy cars driven by cherubic older black women in some sort of a maid's uniform, picking up a little white child.

Memphis is clearly a city owned by white people. If you are a black person in Memphis with any sort of aspirations to better yourself, you set your sights on Chicago, Washington D.C., Atlanta, or the like. Not Memphis. Given all this, it's no wonder that blacks didn't want to spend their discretionary Sunday morning time with whites at our church. I soon caught on that our multiethnic church was white owned too.

CHAPTER 15

A Culture of Honor

When our church began, I was the only piece of chocolate in a room of twenty-six people. By the time I left, we were a body of several thousand, and about 35 percent of the attenders were minority folk. We had begun to woo people of color into our doors. I could always tell first-time guests who were African Americans though. They would come in suited and booted, never greeting me by my first name, but with the honorific title of "Pastor."

The black culture, like many minority cultures, is one of honor. If I ever wanted to awaken the ire of Karen Loritts (my mother), all I had to do was to call some adult by their first name. It was always "Pastor Conley," "Mrs. Johnson," "Deacon Dixon," "Uncle Herman" (though we shared no DNA; he was just a good friend of the family). The black church always attaches a handle to a person's name. I can't tell you how many times I've erroneously been called "Doctor"—a misstep I never correct—by some well-intentioned black pastor or congregant. When historically you've been called "boy" or "nigger" all week or even ignored, it's great to find a refuge of dignity in which now you're called "deacon," "mother," "evangelist," or "pastor."

Our white friends don't do this, and it is more than okay—though I refuse to allow any five-year-old to call me by my first name, but that's another story. I am not here to critique culture, and *white* is not a four-letter word. But I often find myself grieving over the loss of minority

84

culture within the multiethnic church. It's the same old story played in slow motion: (1) minority family comes to church dressed up and calling me "Pastor Loritts"; (2) minority family begins dressing down and calling me "Pastor Bryan"; (3) minority family wears Crocs and calls me Bryan.

Dr. Korie Edwards spends her time researching multiethnic churches. She's a Jesus-loving sociologist who teaches at the Ohio State University. Her research has unearthed something I've always innately grieved{ *minorities look for permission for what's acceptable from whites in a multiethnic environment.*[20] }

Her words cause me to reflect on moments when I've gone to another gear in preaching—you know, that "he got up early Sunday morning" gear. After the message, I could count on an African American saying to me, "Oh, Bryan [or "Pastor," depending on how long they've been coming], "I almost shouted." I'd ask why they didn't—it's biblical to shout, you know. Let the redeemed of the Lord say so, right? Without saying anything more, I understood. They looked around and got the memo: white folks don't do that, and because I'm a guest in their house, neither can I. White Owned.

This does lead to the question of fairness, which is beyond appropriate. Our white siblings weren't pulling aside the new minority family dressed in their suits and wing tips, whispering in their ears to stop dressing like that. Nor did they coach them on what to call the pastor. It's just another instance of our white friends not being aware of their ethnic accent and the power it wields. But none of this did anything to assuage the silent anger festering in my soul. I was becoming aware of an ugly reality. Though I was the lead pastor of this church, I was clearly sharecropping on land I didn't own—a land owned by white folks.

CHAPTER 16

Under the Surface

White evangelicalism insists on normalizing her theological interpretations and erecting them as the standard by which Christianity is authenticated, preaching is evaluated, and church membership is vetted.

Because white evangelicalism is ignorant of her whiteness, her theology is seen as the standard bearer to which everyone must bow. A refusal to do so comes at your own peril. When white evangelicalism is through with you, she calls you a liberal—her version of some four-letter expletive—and sends you packing. We need white evangelicals; we don't need *white evangelicalism*. That thing must die.

To maintain its seat at the head of the table, white evangelicalism must be in control; it needs power. If white evangelicals are not in power, they won't choose to be present in any substantive measures. They won't join our churches or go to conferences historically attended by different ethnicities. *They must be in power.*

In our age of diversity, this is a bit of a problem for white evangelicalism. So to avoid becoming a stench to the world, she works more behind the scenes and is becoming increasingly comfortable allowing minorities to have more of an appearance of power without being fully empowered. NFL owners are happy to draft a minority athlete for the quarterback position and pay him millions while they lurk behind the shadows of their suite. But when said minority steps out of his little box and kneels for justice, he gets "Kaepernicked"—reminded all over again that while he is the face, the owner is, well, the owner; everyone else is just a bunch of millionaire "SOB"s.

This is nothing other than sharecropping. People of color, and mainly blacks, did this for years. As you drove down a Southern highway, it was nothing to see some black man working a plot of land, and if you didn't know better, you would assume that he owned the land. But you knew better. This was white folks' land, where they had developed a system to keep him and his family indebted and dependent for life. Isabel Wilkerson points out in her landmark work, *The Warmth of Other Suns*, that it was only under the cover of night at the risk of one's life that most sharecroppers could leave.[21]

As the years clicked by in Memphis, I found myself becoming increasingly agitated. Why was I getting so frustrated over a minority family's cessation of the use of "Pastor" when addressing me? Why was I growing weary of the umpteenth black woman's confession of "almost shouting"? Why had my irritation over a white family walking out in the middle of my sermonic pleas for justice turned into bitterness? And why was I nauseated at my tenth anniversary when the elders gave me a thank-you gift only after I asked about it some weeks later? Shouldn't I just be happy with the thousands who were coming? Was I acting like some sort of a childish prima donna? While I'm sure there was arrogance and a sense of "I deserve more" lurking beneath the hood of my heart, I was getting restless with sharecropping.

My own journey, in tandem with countless consulting calls and visits with other churches, has given me a look at the inner workings of multiethnic churches. Many of them have diverse boards, but it's here that I'm seeing not just sharecropping dynamics at play but a sort of plantation politics emerging as well.

The church governance model I've always adhered to is an elder-led church. Of course, one can subscribe to a different model of leadership and fit snugly within the realm of orthodoxy, but I've always gone the route of elders. As I tell people in our covenant partners class (for new members), "Whenever a Christian is vetting a potential church, always ask the power question." As the police officer said in the Spike Lee–directed *Malcolm X*, "That's too much power for one man to have." Power should be divided equitably among a group of godly elders. At least that's what I believe.

But here's where it gets a little dicey. Multiethnic churches should have multiethnic boards. If I could sit down with myself a decade and a half ago, I'd say a godly elder board isn't enough. Neither is a diverse godly elder board sufficient. What's really needed is an equitable eldership where each person is confident in the sum total of who they are (spiritually and racially) and has no qualms about speaking truth to power.

What I'm getting at here is a subtlety that many a leader of a multiethnic church has encountered. If white men who are successful in the marketplace in their white-collar jobs serve on the same board as minority men who are not as successful or are too enamored of or intimated by whiteness, that church is white owned. I don't care how dark and woke the lead pastor is, if these are the elder dynamics, he's sharecropping.

During the rash of news stories about black men dying at the hands of white cops, I was called by a person of color who was leading a multiethnic church. I seemed to be able to hear his pulse as he desperately pleaded for my help. At the insistence of his elders, he was instructed not to use the phrase "black lives matter"; instead, he was told to say, "All lives matter." "It was the weirdest thing though," he told me, reflecting on the board meeting where this mandate was issued. "The minority leaders could not look me in the eye as the white chairman was talking."

What became obvious was that his frustration stemmed not so much from the mandate but from the lack of advocates among people of color on the elder board. It seemed as if they had been hypnotized with a zombie-like compliance reminiscent of that of the black folks in the film *Get Out*. It was here that it hit him—he thought he was leading when instead he was nothing more than a sharecropper.

CHAPTER 17

Deeding the Land Back to Jesus

If we are going to make any headway in the multiethnic church, white folks need to deed "the land" back to Jesus. It's not *their* church; it's *his*. At ground zero, this means our white siblings must go out of their way to create an inclusive environment where everyone is free to be who they redemptively are in Christ.

One of the most comedic episodes of Scripture is the scene in which Paul is on his way to be with some Jews. In his company is a young man named Timothy, who is the son of a Jewish mother but a Gentile father. He's yet to be circumcised, and Paul, knowing this, doesn't want to be offensive to Timothy's Jewish family. So he tells Timothy he should get circumcised as a way of showing a deferential honor to the Jews (Acts 16:3).

Was this absolutely necessary? No. Remember, Paul was vociferous in his conviction that Gentiles need not be circumcised to be considered Christian. He spoke in explicit language against any hint of this being a requirement. But what concerns Paul at this point is not Timothy's Christianity but that Timothy not be an impediment to the work of God. So Paul has him subjugate the Gentile dimension of his anatomy to honor the ethnically other.

This is what's needed when we speak of deeding the land of the multiethnic church back to God and thereby emancipating Jesus from his white evangelical captivity. For years, minorities have acquiesced to white cultural demands. We have answered to "boy," refused to look them in the eyes, walked on the other side of the street, sat in the far recesses of the bus, drunk out of substandard water fountains, and picked up our food on the other side of the chicken joint.

Given all this, you'll forgive me for rolling my eyes if you say calling your minority leader "pastor" is too much to ask. Neither is sitting in lament while hearing a hard message on historical racism instead of charging the pulpit to argue with the minority preacher as soon as he says, "Amen." Lifting your hands past your shoulders may cut against the grain of your Presbyterian upbringing, but if it green-lights the minority person sitting a few seats down to freely worship the way they're culturally conditioned, then this is a form of Zacchaen restitution.

If as a minority you are too enamored with whiteness and are asked to serve on an elder board, you will continue the legacy of sharecropping multiethnic churches. We need Jesus-loving minorities who will speak truth to power and help maintain the health of the elder board. Much has been made of renegade pastors, but too little has been said by way of commentary on elder boards gone wild.

Renegade elders encased in white skin serving in a multiethnic context amongst minority elders who are paralyzed by white idolization will only lengthen the sharecropping contract. Instead, we need Jesus-loving minorities with a steeled resolve encased in love. Or as my friend Dr. Barry Corey says, we need people who love kindness, people with firm convictions but soft edges. Plus, some robust back-and-forth in an elder room is often good medicine. Any expert in the field of group dynamics will tell you that contrarian thinking and conflict are signs of health among teams.

The shelf life of minority leaders pushing hard for reconciliation and justice on white evangelicalism's land is short. They will either sell their souls and settle into a life of sharecropping, walk off the land and become bitter, or lovingly opt for genuine equity in the very land they're working, where they are accountable stewards and not indentured servants. There needs to be an uprising for the latter.

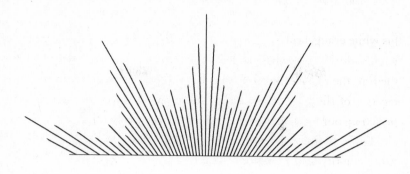

Kaepernicked

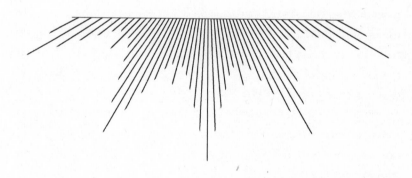

CHAPTER 18

Anatomy of a Church Split

In the early part of the twentieth century, the white church was split in two. On the one side were Christians who said that Christianity at its core is about a relationship with God and a search for truth. On the other side, Christians said that to follow Jesus means to love one's neighbor, thus propelling them to emphasize justice. When the great church divorce of the early twentieth century occurred, sending the fundamentalist father in one direction and the modernist mother in the other, black folks refused to choose parental sides. This is a point that Dr. Mary Beth Mathews excavates in her book *Doctrine and Race: African American Evangelicals and Fundamentalism Between the Wars*.[22]

My forefathers did not have the luxury of deciding between doctrinal orthodoxy and cultural engagement. Held captive by a culture where lynching was the order of the day, denied the right to vote, and treated as less than human, African Americans en masse opted for a robust theology while donning the well-worn shoe leather of an intense orthopraxy.

"Gospel-centered preaching" is not some new phenomenon introduced by our Calvinist friends in the early twenty-first century. The black church was doing that since its inception, seeing every sermon as a *kairotic* moment to sprint to the cross. In the black tradition, one has not preached until Jesus has been unveiled. Nowhere was this more manifest than in the pulpit of the venerable African-American preacher Gardner

Taylor, who had inscribed on the floor behind the pulpit, for himself and for every guest preacher to see, the words of John 12, reminding them as they preached, "We would see Jesus" (John 12:21 KJV).

Coupled with orthodoxy, the black church fully embraced the delightful burden of caring for its own. We developed our own community development corporations, oftentimes without going through any sort of bureaucratic formalities. We adopted orphans, cared for the poor, and became a safe refuge for those who had migrated from the bowels of the Deep South to the urban cities of the north and west during the great migration. Isabel Wilkerson comments that it was during this period of mass migration that many black churches organized auxiliaries named after the states people had left so they could find a sense of community and belonging.[23]

And who could forget that during the civil rights movement it was the black church that served as an incubator where marchers gathered, accruing the much-needed spiritual sustenance required to protest in the streets, knowing they'd eventually land in jail. And once in jail it was often the black church that raised funds for bail and looming legal fees. Simply put, if we did not care for our own, who else would?

But this hardly tells the whole story. Beyond the black church, ethnocentric immigrant churches continue to provide ballast and a safe harbor for weary souls coming to American shores. I often surprise people by telling them I have never believed that every church should be multiethnic. Churches should match their community, and even beyond this, there is a place for immigrant churches that provide a meaningful point of entry into our great country and allow people to connect with God by worshiping and hearing God's Word through their heart language.

By the time my family and I anchored in Memphis, my spiritual formation had welded together orthodoxy with orthopraxy, exegesis with activism, and vertical reconciliation to God with horizontal reconciliation with neighbor, no matter their color or class. I would soon discover that not everyone held my worldview, and it would be my responsibility to lift up the light of God's Word so the Holy Spirit could illumine them.

CHAPTER 19

Begin with Orthodoxy, Conclude with Orthopraxy

The children of white evangelicalism have a propensity toward a theological kind of entitlement. Kay Wills Wyma in her book *Cleaning House* describes how entitlement happens when we consume without contributing.[24] As the offspring of fundamentalism, conservative evangelicalism has long loved her prophecy conferences, Bible studies, and family camps—accompanied by celebrity teachers—where a culture of consumption has bequeathed to her a genetic predisposition toward spiritual obesity.

Yet her consumption has historically been devoid of a contributive activism, thus causing her to be entitled. If the impetus for the divorce was fundamentalists wanting to hold fast to the truth, then there was bound to be a gorging of sorts at the table of God's Word, resulting in a just condemnation that they are hearers but not doers of said Word in all of its magnificent facets.

And while any historian will point out the mission-mindedness of white evangelicalism, this was nothing more than *spiritual* colonization, where souls were cared for, while bodies and felt needs went generally neglected. Sure, there's been a recent tidal wave of urban engagement seen in the new vocabulary of such phrases as *incarnational living*, *missional communities*, and the like; yet it cannot be denied that this is recent and not historical. Outlier examples always exist, but these exceptions prove the rule that white evangelicalism has historically been more concerned with *knowing* right than *doing* what's right, especially with respect to the ethnically other.

If you are searching for proof of the entitlement associated with the offspring of white evangelicalism, notice how many people bristle when asked to engage in issues of cross-ethnic justice. Watch the anger some of them display when a minority preacher reminds them of their historic culpability in systemic injustice, gathering in a three-point stance as the preacher concludes so they can bombard him with their theological justifications. And when we talk of proactively seeking minorities for certain positions, catch the hesitation and pushback as they cry, "Unfair."

As one who has raised teenagers, I know entitlement when I see it. They love watching television but hate contributing to the well-being of the house by taking out the garbage or raking leaves. Teenagers hate to be inconvenienced. Many are consummate consumers. Consuming is easy; contributing is something altogether different. The children of white evangelicalism have been paralyzed by a perpetual adolescence.

I discovered these things the hard way when we set anchor in Memphis. Almost immediately, I was chastised by my white brothers and sisters for preaching a "social gospel." It didn't take me long to realize how that phrase was code for *liberal* and *unbiblical*. My reflex reaction was to dig in and fight back, but this is not why I had come to Memphis. If I were to pastor my white parishioners, I had to divest myself of any vestiges of white idolization and fear and with great Pauline courage and patience show them "the most excellent way" (1 Corinthians 12:31).

My years at Bible college and seminary equipped me to see that there was a way to approach this, but I would need to take a few steps back in my preaching. If the way to a man's heart is through his stomach, then the best route to eulogizing white evangelicalism is by showing her members the plain truth of Scripture that their whiteness had blinded them to.

Despite all of her shortcomings, white evangelicalism has maintained a high view of Scripture. This was to be my "in" with them. As I counsel any pastor who is seeking to transition a church into a multiethnic trajectory, never begin by preaching on race relations; always begin by *preaching the gospel*. Soon enough, congregants will see that the two are inextricably linked.

When our Lord was crucified, it happened, of course, upon a cross. The cross was constructed of two beams, one vertical and the other horizontal. The vertical beam was rooted deeply into the ground, thereby providing support and stability. The horizontal beam was tethered to the vertical one, making both beams essential for his death and our salvation. What is true in the natural is also true in the spiritual. The validity and vibrancy of our faith necessitate a staunch refusal of the either/or dichotomy that the church of the early twentieth century settled for, and it demands the both/and approach that our Lord and Savior espoused. The gospel is *both* vertical and horizontal.

Now, Paul is clear when he says that our vertical reconciliation to God is "of first importance" (1 Corinthians 15:3). There can never be any true reconciliation horizontally without our first being vertically reconciled to God. This is a point our modernist friends missed. Truth must be firmly buttressed in God; without this, we are but a stone's throw away from doctrinal error and spiritual malpractice.

Any fair reading of the Bible will reveal the conjoining of the vertical and horizontal dimensions of our faith. In Matthew 22:37–40, Jesus said that the greatest commandment is to love the Lord our God with the totality of our being (vertical) and to love our neighbor as ourselves (horizontal). In 1 John 4:20, the apostle John posed the rhetorical question of how we can claim to love God, whom we don't see (vertical), while hating our brother or sister, whom we do see (horizontal).

In Ephesians 2, Paul begins with vertical reconciliation when he says that the Christ follower has been saved by grace through faith, and not by works. Yet for so many years in the halls of white evangelicalism, I never once heard a sermon on the rest of Ephesians 2, leaving me to think there were really only ten verses in the chapter. But right on the heels of our vertical reconciliation, Paul talks about the ethnic implications when he says that Jesus' death has taken a sledgehammer to the dividing wall of hostility, allowing Jews and Gentiles to rush in together and worship as one family. Seen against the backdrop of the totality of the Pauline corpus, Ephesians 2 is merely a microcosm of the vertical and horizontal aspects of our faith.

In almost every letter, Paul begins with orthodoxy and concludes with orthopraxy, with doctrine and then duty, and much of the orthopraxy has to do with the horizontal accoutrements of the cross—how we relate to one another. The Bible knows nothing of a vertical reconciliation that is not evident in horizontal reconciliation with others. An unforgiving Christian is an oxymoron. So is a racist one.

But we haven't pushed the envelope far enough. We must ask the question, "Who exactly was Paul writing to as he revealed the vertical and horizontal elements of our faith?" My own reading of Acts left me winded, wondering why I had never heard these things in my New Testament Survey classes. Read it for yourself. When Paul walks into a city he asks two questions: (1) Where is the synagogue?—because he wants to preach the gospel to the Jews—and (2) Where do the Gentiles hang out?—because he wants to reach them.

These questions arise out of Paul's missiological philosophy of ministry seen in Romans 1:16: "For I am not ashamed of the gospel, because it is the power of God that brings salvation to everyone who believes: first to the Jew, then to the Gentile." If you grew up in the church, you no doubt heard this verse—and maybe even were forced to find it quickly in some sword drill competition—but don't see it so much with evangelistic eyes (though appropriate to do so) as with sociological ones. Paul was not ashamed of the gospel, because to him it represented God's power to *both* Jews and Greeks, the very ones Paul was called to comprehensively reach.

With conversions happening rapidly among both groups, Paul does not go the pragmatic route, starting two churches for the two distinct ethnicities. This would have been the easy thing to do, of course, but Paul would have none of it. To Paul, vertical reconciliation required nothing less than horizontal reconciliation, and the theater in which this was to be enacted was the local church. In case you missed it, most of Paul's churches were multiethnic, which is exactly why he deals with such issues as food and circumcision. If Paul was ever asked if the gospel was social, he would nod his head yes, like a bobblehead doll.

These are gospel issues. Is the gospel social? Of course it is. Like the word *evangelical*, the term *social gospel* has become politicized. But any fair reading of the text of Scripture will uncover the social implications of the gospel. Because Christ first loved us, we are to love others (1 Corinthians 13). Having been forgiven by God, we are to forgive (Matthew 18:21–35). Having been reconciled to God through the bloody cross, we are to, as best we can, live at peace with all people (Romans 12:18). And the generosity of Jesus extended at Calvary is to inspire generosity among his followers toward the marginalized (Matthew 21:33–46). There is no getting around the social requirements of the gospel.

CHAPTER 20

The Cost of Discipleship

It was the pastor-theologian Karl Barth who, when asked about his philosophy of preaching, stated that he merely takes the Bible in one hand and the newspaper in the other. Barth was concerned not only with exegeting a text but also with exegeting the culture and showing how the former came to bear on the latter. Faithful preaching is never satisfied with a sermonic lecture in which the pastor in some form or fashion shouts, "It means! It means! It means! Let's pray." Who cares about a twenty-minute history lesson on the Jebusites if one cannot show how it connects to the single dad whose heart is broken over the demise of his marriage and family. It is the preacher who bears the joyful burden of connecting the roads of ancient Jebus to the streets of modern Memphis.

In some sense, my work of mining the truths of Scripture and exposing our mostly white church to the magnetism between the vertical and horizontal dimensions of the gospel was the easy part. What was hard was mustering up the courage to show them how that truth played out in the lives of early twenty-first-century Memphians. That was where I ran the risk of getting "Kaepernicked."

As I mentioned earlier, there exists within the city of Memphis a country club that does not allow African Americans to join. Well, to be fair, they do have one member who lives in another state, but we all know what that's about. I was invited to play there, and against my senses, I gave in. When the round was over, I felt as if my soul needed a ladle full of hand sanitizer—I felt that gross. I vowed never to play there again.

Sure enough, many of our church members had grown up at the club and still enjoyed their memberships there. What would Paul and the Scriptures say to this? So taking my Bible and my "newspaper" with me, I gathered up all the prophetic courage I could muster and used by way of application the social implications of the gospel. "If you are merely using your membership at this restrictive club as a means of enjoyment and do not see it as an opportunity for reformation, this is sin," I sermonically implored one Sunday. My words caused a bit of a stir among the white parishioners, and I spent the better part of the next couple of weeks meeting with several of them, who expressed their frustration over my "careless remarks." Mind you, these were thirty-somethings who had grown up in churches in Memphis but had never been challenged by those churches over the injustices they were nursing.

Prophetic courage must never be wielded in discrimination to induce white guilt. Preachers must be equitable in their pleas for justice. Jesus called out sin in both the woman caught in adultery and "that fox" Herod, one of the rulers of his day. I had to be careful to not turn my Memphian pulpit into a pep rally for blacks. There were times when they needed to be rebuked as well.

Lawrence Otis Graham points out in his book *Our Kind of People* the elitism of the African-American middle to upper middle class.[25] There is this Jeffersonian sense in which once we've made it "on up to the east side,"[26] we ain't never looking back. By far the most difficult people to engage in compassion projects at our church were my African-American siblings. We once built a home for a black family in need in one of the poorest neighborhoods in Memphis. Of the three hundred people who showed up from our church over the course of six weeks, only three were black. This was wrong—a fact I likewise pointed out on a Sunday morning.

The San Francisco 49ers quarterback Colin Kaepernick probably had some idea that his decision to be a vessel for justice would imperil his career. Kneeling during the national anthem to bring attention to black bodies lying in the streets of Ferguson, Staten Island, Baton Rouge, and the proverbial "Every Town, USA," invoked the ire of many and ultimately set in motion his exile from the league. Once other players joined in and the NFL's capitalistic coffers were threatened, the almost all-white ownership had no choice but to somehow quench the fire that was threatening their livelihoods. Along the way, Colin Kaepernick became the sacrificial lamb.

Every person of color occupying space within white evangelicalism wrestles with an inner Colin Kaepernick. We see injustice, but we know that to speak against it within the context of all-white ownership may very well get us ostracized and unemployed, branded with a scarlet letter. So what are we to do?

My experience under the tyranny of white evangelicalism has exposed me to a lot of coonery. Too many people of color have chosen to "yessuh" and "nossuh" their way up Mount Significance, as they hurriedly try to be liked while hopefully solidifying and extending their brand. So they don't speak to the injustice. At best, they play it safe. They desire the invitations, book deals, and positive image. Far too many people of color have chosen to be like the apostle Peter and switch tables to pacify any suspicions white evangelicalism may hold. Paul could not stomach such coonery. In a tense conversation with Peter, he made it clear that Peter's refusal to stand up for what is right was out of step with the gospel (Galatians 2:11–21).

White evangelicalism has always held a fond affection for the safe person of color. Frederick Douglass was the darling of abolitionists until he decided to marry one of their white daughters. It was then that he discovered he was good enough to be their brother-in-Christ, just not their brother-in-law. Some truths come just a little too close to home.

Many have made assumptions about me. Some white people have told me that they found my views shocking, questioned whether I had gone liberal, and accused me of hating white people. Their surprise may well come from a quick once-over of my educational résumé, pedigree, light skin, and sanguine demeanor, making it easy to conclude that I'd make a fine boy in the home of white evangelicalism. But don't let the smooth taste fool you. I dearly love all people and will labor to my dying day to see the multiethnic church established as the new normal. But I refuse to be bought by anyone. Truth is truth.

Colin Kaepernick's decision to use his platform as an MRI to expose the injustices in our land has cost him millions. But this is a cheap price to pay when compared to Jesus. He spoke truth to power. Jesus pronounced woes on hypocritical Pharisees, dismissed the invitation to sell his soul to Satan, and refused to circumvent the cross by placating Pilate and his questions. Jesus refused to lower the bar of discipleship to accommodate the wealthy and those whom society lifted up as significant. He pointed out the greed of the rich young ruler and the rich landowner.

His behavior would finally get him "Kaepernicked"—caught in a web of collusion spun by the power brokers of his day. Jesus went to his grave perceived by many as an impoverished lunatic who had lost. Yet eternity, as we know, will have the final say.

Any minority preacher immersed in the sea of white evangelicalism who has never been Kaepernicked has not authentically ministered in the messianic lineage he has supposedly inherited. To go the way of Jesus and preach truth to power is to guarantee a Kaepernicking. There is, as Dietrich Bonhoeffer said, a "cost of discipleship"—a truth he heard preached regularly by his black Harlem pastor, Pastor Adam Clayton Powell.

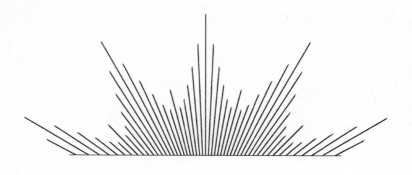

Scouting
Jackie

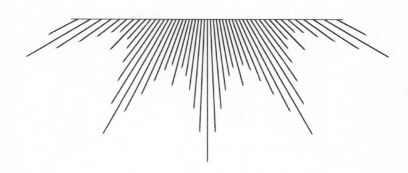

CHAPTER 21

Black Preachers Adrift

I never imagined our church in Memphis accumulating the national recognition she did. But as God continued to breathe on our efforts, the phone began to ring, and I found myself immersed in conversations with young, rising leaders who wanted to know the secret sauce behind our multiethnic success. They were simply amazed that such a thing could happen in the very city where our drum major for justice had been slain. So was I.

Many of these conversations took an unexpected turn. The young minority twentysomething at the other end of the telephone line or across from me at the coffee table wanted to know if I'd be willing to bring them on to serve as a resident for a few years so they could peek under the hood of our church and kick the tires. These requests sobered me, for they caused my mind to drift back more than a decade to when, like them, I sat in Dr. Kenneth Ulmer's office, begging to go on some trip with him, assuring him I'd stay out of his way. I would carry his bags and do whatever. Like the young man who came up to Malcolm X in the diner of Spike Lee's film, I was eager to just be in his presence.

My own experience of being mentored, coupled with the theological moorings of the Great Commission, would not allow me to turn a deaf ear to their pleas. But there was something else at play. I was noticing an ecclesiastical phenomenon within white evangelicalism—*black preachers adrift*.

For African Americans, all roads have historically led back to the black church. While I mourn the reality of this becoming less true with time, it nonetheless has been an undeniable fact. Most R&B groups got their start swaying in some choir, while most black preachers had their oratorical coming-out party spittin' some Easter speech dressed in a white robe, while Big Momma and an assuring crowd cheered them on.

Soon enough, some of these young leaders acknowledge the call to preach and trot off to school, some even opting to enter the halls of white evangelicalism. Once here, they will inevitably learn new things, while most will not have the discernment to eat the meat and throw away the bones. Some will even fall in love with white evangelicalism. Inevitably, many will graduate like I did—critiquing the black church, if not altogether divorcing her. What saved me during my period of separation was walking in close community with black pastors like Bishop Kenneth Ulmer and Dr. Tony Evans. Sadly, not everyone is as fortunate as I was.

Biblical noses pointed nauseatingly toward heaven, these budding black preachers whose ink has barely dried on their degree discover they are ecclesiological orphans. They're faced with a conundrum. Many are too theologically light-skinned to embrace the black church as is, but too theologically dark to be fully embraced the way they feel they should be by the white church. So where are they to go?

They came to me, and I felt the christological impulse to gather them under my wings, as a hen gathers her chicks. So off we went, choosing to start a residency program at our church predominantly populated by black men, many of whom were both biological and ecclesiastical orphans. This would prove to be my most satisfying life's work, as well as my most painful.

CHAPTER 22

Never Saw It Coming

G et life insurance. Stop talking bad about the black church—that will never be tolerated here. Here's how you preach a gospel big enough for National Baptists and Presbyterians. While there will be consequences if you engage in sex with a person outside of marriage, I won't get rid of you. Make all of your big mistakes now, while in your twenties. The cardinal sin here is arrogance; just about anything else we can work through. I'm going to show you what it looks like to love a woman, to engage in the lives of your children, and to be a pastor."

These were lessons I taught our residents in classes, in airport lounges, and at the dinner table at my house. I not only taught them, but like hospitals do with medical residents, I allowed them to practice their craft—in our case, the craft of preaching—under my careful eye at our church—and our people loved it. The process was grueling. First, they had to complete my preaching cohort, where they preached many sermons in a lab-like setting with real-time feedback. We were always brutally honest. Some were shaken to the core and moved to tears. In every class, I could count on having to deliver the news to one person that this was not their calling. While it was hard for them to hear, I've always believed the greatest gift you can give a young twentysomething is the gift of self-discovery. The sooner they find out why they were created, the better. Too many people wake up in their late thirties with the awful sensation of being trapped—making money doing something they can do but were never created to do.

If they made it through the cohort and I sensed a real call, I gave them a date months in advance to preach to our whole church. They had to write out their sermon, and I reviewed it. Once I approved, they preached it to our staff in an *American Idol* type setting, where seated around the conference room were a few Simon Cowells. If the staff gave them the thumbs-up, they preached on a Sunday morning, followed the next day by all of us as a cohort watching the sermon and providing feedback. They often remarked how they felt like fraternity pledges. For those who survived this subtle hazing, there was immense satisfaction.

A few years later, having graduated from our cohort, they were off and running, always taking the time to thank me for the investment— something they didn't have to do. In my mind, I was simply paying down on the tab I had opened with the likes of Dr. Tony Evans, Dr. Kenneth Ulmer, and Dr. Gordon Kirk.

Whatever satisfaction they experienced after graduating from our residency couldn't even approach what I felt. In hindsight, I knew that God was using me to gift back to the church a generation of young minority leaders who had solid theology effervescing out of a healthy ethnic identity. Over the course of a strenuous couple of years, these leaders had their ethnicity gifted back to them after having it pillaged in the halls of white evangelicalism. So they emerged with a robust theology devoid of any coonery, lovingly steeled in their commitment to be vessels of prophetic courage. But as it turned out, I am so sorry for what I did to them. I never saw it coming. Little did I realize that I had set them up for seasons of rejection and disappointment.

CHAPTER 23

The Next Bryan Loritts

Word leaked out about our residency program, and I soon began to entertain a different kind of phone call. Well-intentioned white leaders, who didn't mean an ounce of condescension, began to ask, "Where can I find the next Bryan Loritts?" Flattered and somewhat put off by their question, I knew what they were getting at.

When we began our church in 2003, no one was really talking much about the multiethnic church, at least not the way they are today. Statistics bear this out. At the dawn of the twenty-first century, less than 3 percent of all Protestant churches qualified as multiethnic. Today that number has moved to somewhere between 10 and 14 percent. Everyone, it seems, is at least raising the question of diversity when it comes to the church.

One doesn't need to spend a day in seminary to realize that *leadership* is key to pulling off a multiethnic church, but it's here where a problem comes into view. Churches mirror our relationships. If people are still coming to church primarily out of the relationships they've nurtured with people in the church, then sanctuaries reflect dinner tables. When any leader who aspires to move a church in a multiethnic direction asks where they can find a certain minority leader to match the demographic they want to pursue, this is often a telling indictment of the social circles that the leader has traveled in.

So I found myself playing the role of a baseball scout commissioned to find the next wave of talent for the major leagues. I was being asked to discover the next Jackie Robinson—the minority leader who was competent, but who also had the kind of wiring that could endure the insensitivities bound to come their way as they settled into their seat as the first, and often the only, minority leader in the lonely world of the majority church.

My grandfather played in the Negro leagues. Old "Hambone," they called him. I could never get my arms around the reason for this nickname, but Pop-Pop was hardly bashful when regaling us with tales of his exploits on the diamond. There was a glimmer in his eye as he reminisced about legends like Josh Gibson, Satchel Paige, and a host of other Negro league stars. And while I found some of his stories hard to believe—like how for practice he would chase down rabbits in an open field to develop his speed—he never spoke of that era in his life with sadness. To hear him talk, playing in the Negro leagues wasn't second-class citizenship. If his voice betrayed any trace of melancholy, it was when he commented that the leagues no longer existed.

Branch Rickey was a major accomplice in the death of the Negro leagues. His decision to draft Jackie Robinson was a double-edged sword. The first time Jackie took the field, the Dodger organization gained a host of chocolate fans from all over the country, and yet most of these same fans knew that the hourglass had been flipped over and the expiration date on their beloved leagues was closing in on them.

Sure enough, major league scouts began to pillage our beloved leagues, taking away the best we had to offer. In Jackie's wake came one-named legends like Willie, Satchel, and Hank. My people traded in stadiums where they could sit wherever they liked for sitting in restricted areas in some of the major league stadiums. There is a cost to integration.

I don't know how many African-American scouts there were back then in the employ of the major leagues, if any at all, but I do know I was becoming a scout for a different "major league" of sorts—the white church. With eager "Branch Rickeys" dialing me up from all over the country, I began to feel like I was mining the black church of her best and brightest talent.

CHAPTER 24

The Price Tag of Diversity

There's a price tag to diversity. Just ask the Little Rock Nine or any minority firsts to walk through the doors of all-white educational facilities. Generations and an institution removed from legislated busing, well-meaning white leaders tend to forget this. So had I.

My years of leading a residency at our church in Memphis, coupled with my position in the small world of African-American evangelicals (a position I inherited because of my father), had put me at the center of one of the most desirable social nexuses in the age of aspiring diverse churches and organizations. White leaders from across the country began to put me on their speed dial, wanting me to broker their hiring of Jackie. Almost immediately, I began to sense that something was wrong.

One of the first calls I fielded was from a church in Mississippi, perched right on the outskirts of a growing urban center. Sensing the tidal wave of change coming their way, they decided to embark on a bold move and hire the first minority pastor in the history of their church. I must give them credit. They had partially done their homework. They knew that not any old minority preacher would do; it had to be one who matched the demographic that was well represented in their community but absent from their building. He needed to be African American. I was new at this and didn't ask a ton of questions, but I did inquire whether this position entailed at least a modicum of

preaching—to which they said that it would. I made a few recommen-
dations, and some days later, they reached out to Kelton, one of my sons
in the ministry.

Kelton kept me aware of what was going on in the hiring process,
and when they got to the financial package, we were both surprised to
discover the church asked him to raise about 25 percent of his salary.
When he ran it by me, I told him that it didn't feel good, but Kelton
had just graduated from seminary and our residency and was eager to
settle in with his young bride to his first full-time ministry assignment.
So off they went.

Of course, our church helped supplement some of the support he
was being asked to raise, but Kelton really struggled to get the requisite
funds. Raising support is a daunting task for just about everyone, but
especially those who are descendants of slaves. Any statistical marker
will reveal the close connection between ethnicity and the economic
gap. While my ancestors provided free labor, our white slave masters
were able to earn a lot of money. While my grandparents lived from
paycheck to paycheck during the tyranny of Jim Crow, our white
siblings continued to accrue more wealth. Sure, it goes without saying
that not every white person is rich, but compared to the average black
person, they are. As my friend Lecrae says, these are just "the facts."

This presents more than a challenge to the descendants of those
once regarded as chattel. On average, we don't have a grandmother who
can write the big checks, an uncle who can chip in, or a distant cousin
sitting on a gold mine. Look at just about every nonprofit Christian
organization whose model is predicated on raising support, and you
will see a deficit of black folks. This is just one of many reasons white
evangelicalism persists unchecked. Excuse my grammar, but we ain't
got it like that.

Languishing in his endeavor to raise support, Kelton began to
experience problems at home. Like a submarine descending to the
depths, financial difficulties can place extreme amounts of pressure on
a marriage relationship, and Kelton and his wife were no exception.

Heeding my counsel, he asked the church to reconsider their agreement. They dug in and said it would be unfair—after all, what kind of message would this communicate to some of the other staff who also had to raise support? Feeling as if he was about to sink under the financial stress, Kelton asked me to talk to his pastor.

Some days later, I was on a call with Kelton's pastor. I listened patiently while given news I already knew: (1) Kelton wasn't the only one to raise support; (2) Kelton knew what he was getting into before he was hired; and (3) it would be unfair to lessen the demands.

Sensing that my colleague had finished making his case, I chimed in. Fairness is a desired virtue, but it doesn't work if the system has been historically unfair to the point where we still feel its vibrations some centuries later. As winsomely as I could, I appealed to a unique opportunity this pastor had to provide gospel-inspired restitution in the lineage of Zacchaeus. His silence told me everything. The best he could muster was that he would run it by his elders.

I never heard how this went, and neither did Kelton. Unable to secure funding, he took a part-time job to supplement his income. The church responded in a viciously passive-aggressive way by reducing his status to part-time. With no benefits and a now pregnant wife, Kelton slipped out the back door. She's embittered. He's delivering packages. Last we talked, he still knows that God wants him in some sort of vocational ministry, but if it does happen . . . if it's up to him . . . it will be in an all-black setting.

CHAPTER 25

Let's Just Say It
Didn't Go Well

W hat do you think?" Jason asked me.
   "How much preaching will you get to do? After all,
preaching is what God's put in you," I responded.

"They said there will be some, but we haven't worked out the
amount."

"Okay, but make sure you get clarity on this."

I've got to give it to the new white church Jason went to work for
in the Midwest suburb. They let him preach, almost immediately. Like
many of the men I helped to place, Jason was the first African-American
pastor to serve on staff in the history of this church. The senior pastor
was a man full of holy ambition and godly character. I had known of
him from my years of itinerant preaching and had never heard a bad
word said about him. His only fault, as I would come to learn, was he
had what Paul called a "zeal . . . not based on knowledge" (Romans 10:2).

Jason sat in his pastor's office talking through his first sermon and
what the pastor had in mind. The congregation needed to be challenged
on racism and painted a vision for what biblical—or as he would say,
"gospel-centered"—reconciliation looked like. This was exactly what
Jason had signed up for. So a few weeks later, Jason eagerly took his
text and let it rip.

Let's just say things didn't go too well. The almost all-white audience was quiet, and you could see them turning a collective red. They fidgeted in their seats and fumbled with their phones. Some anxiously got up and in a sprinter's walk made their way to the parking lot, where moments later, angry text messages began to boil up in the senior pastor's in-box. A few even called a meeting with the senior pastor in which they kindly threatened to take their ample finances and go to the next church if things weren't amended.

Jason was never reprimanded. His sermon was never reviewed or critiqued. In fact, no one said a single word to him about it. Knowing Jason as I do, he was probably way too abrasive with the audience. He tends to come at things with a prophetic aggression, when a white audience with virgin ears to this subject needed a pastoral touch. But if you think providing not so flattering feedback on a sermon is already tough, mix in the race dynamic, and you can readily see why Jason's pastor chose the path of silence.

Jason never preached again at the church, and all the while, he was left wondering, *What happened?*

An autopsy on Jason's time at the church would reveal one significant cause for the ministerial catastrophe he endured: Jason walked into a congregation ill-prepared for all of him, and by this, I mean the *black him*.

Sociologists are careful to tease out the differences between ethnicity and culture. Within every ethnicity, there are at least three major cultures. In other words, *black* is not monolithic. Neither are all Koreans or Irish (or any other ethnicity). One of the cultural stratifications embedded within each ethnicity is what I label "C3" in my book *Right Color, Wrong Culture*.[27] A C3 is a person who is culturally inflexible, who refuses to adjust.

We see this in the Bible with the Pharisees, who were ethnic Jews but culturally inflexible. We also see it in Acts 6 with the cultural collision between the Hellenistic and Hebraic Jews. The Hebraic Jews were C3s. Most whites in America are C3s, since they have been raised in a country where the white way of thinking and approaching life is still considered normative and mainstream.

The problem arises when a C2 (a person who is culturally flexible and not ethnically hostile) or a C3 of another ethnicity like Jason comes into an environment and begins to point out blind spots in less than flattering ways. This causes a sense of corporate disequilibrium if that church or organization hasn't been carefully prepared. In most cases, the resulting stress prompts a fight-or-flight response. Unwilling to deal with members whose feet are dangling on the edge of departure, most pastors choose to pacify the demands of their constituency, sacrificing the Jasons of the world on the altar of their passivity. Jason had been sent into the battlefield of race with no one to provide protective cover from the rounds being silently fired his way by the people.

While the Jasons of the world should preach on topics like race under the watchful guidance of their senior pastor, it is the senior pastor who must prepare the ground for the people to receive them. We see this in the Bible. In the book of Acts, when a dramatic shift is about to be made in the economy of God by the pouring out of the Holy Spirit on the Gentiles en masse, God readies the soil of their hearts. Acts 10 is the story of God preparing both Peter and Cornelius for a historic move. Jewish Peter just doesn't show up one day to Gentile Cornelius's house to announce the gospel. A lot of behind-the-scenes work has already occurred.

The same can be said a couple of chapters earlier when a Jew gets into the chariot of a very powerful black man, and a gospel-driven multiethnic exchange takes place. God knows the principalities and powers involved in the dynamics of race, so he spends ample time cultivating the soil before he dispenses the seed. How much more so should we!

My fingers have paused somewhat as I consider this point. Part of me feels as if I'm letting Jason's former pastor off the hook too easily. Now I don't really know him and I've never been to his church, but I would venture to guess, in the strongest of terms, that this man knows that whenever a major new initiative is ready to be introduced at a church, ample time should be spent in meetings and in preaching—all in an effort to prepare the people to see the vision and run with it. This just seems to be Leadership 101. So why did this not happen with the inflammable topic of race? Many of the senior pastors I know have a PhD in leadership but tend to be kindergartners when it comes to issues of ethnicity.

A deficit of courage is the only plausible explanation. Jason's pastor chose to outsource the topic to his new African-American hire, while he went off on vacation that Sunday. His "courage account" revealed insufficient funds when some of his white constituency threatened to leave, and not once did he do the heavy lifting of shepherding by having Jason's back. Instead, his silence, coupled with the banishment of Jason from the pulpit, affirmed his congregants' complaints. It was the senior pastor's way of saying, "I'm sorry, and this will never happen again." White evangelicalism had won the day.

My friend Dr. Korie Edwards explains how attending homogenous churches actually entrenches racism. Because we all carry our own biases and presuppositions (many of which are ethnically informed), we need people around us who don't see things the way we do and can offer a yin-and-yang type of friction to challenge our worldviews. When this doesn't happen and we opt to immerse ourselves in a sea of people who generally see it the way we do—refusing to allow our biases to be challenged—these biases are affirmed and deepened.

It is here where white evangelicalism intensifies its grip on the local church and becomes especially pernicious when a church wants to move into a multiethnic trajectory. What were many of the white congregants of Jason's church communicating as their faces turned red and angry emails were sent? They were saying that the home team here is white, not black. There's just no avoiding this conclusion. The white way of doing church and reading the Bible had been established as the normative standard by which everything was evaluated, measured, and filtered. When Jason defied their categories, he was weighed and found wanting. White evangelicalism had won the day.

Part of what made the first wave of churches in the Bible so beautiful was their *diversity*. There was ethnic diversity, along with class diversity. Jew and Gentile, rich and poor, were coming together. There was no ethnic or cultural home team in the first church. In fact, the only place one could go in the Roman Empire and see substantive exchanges among men and women, rich and poor, Jew and Gentile—experiences of what the writers of the New Testament call *koinonia*—was the local church.

In a society predicated on class—on a caste system of sorts—the church defied all of these odds. But the church is not some sort of utopia devoid of problems. To experience what Dr. Korie Edwards calls "the elusive dream,"[28] we need courageous leaders who will not pawn off the hard work of transitioning a church in this direction, but instead will choose to lock arms and even risk losing people so that the dream can come to fruition.

Reduced to a mere token staff member who regularly gave the church's announcements, Jason hung in there for another eighteen months or so. Quietly he made his exit. Last I heard, he was planting a church. No, he hasn't given up on the dream of being a part of something multiethnic; he just realized if it was going to happen, he needed to have power.

CHAPTER 26

The Inescapable
Network of Mutuality

M arriage tends to have archaeological proclivities, with God using my spouse as an archaeologist hammering away at the soil of my heart. Yet what often is unearthed beneath the surface is not a rare treasure, but some repulsive trait that had lain dormant, hidden by the decades of my singleness. I never knew how selfish I was until I shared my life, bed, accounts, and home with Korie. This unsettling truth is rarely embraced at first. Marriage has a way of instigating a fight-or-flight response. But decades into my own marriage, I can vouch for the fact that if one rides it out, choosing the third way of *embrace* instead of fight or flight, it really does get better.

Christian ministry is unique in that we believe the church is not merely an organization or a company, but a family. At least this is how Jesus, Paul, and the leaders of the early church saw things. This is important to remember. When a church decides to hire someone, they are extending an invitation to not merely join a staff but to immerse themselves into what Dr. Scot McKnight calls "a fellowship of differents."[29] As if this isn't weighty enough, the enormity of this exponentially increases when the person brought in is not only a person of a different ethnicity, but someone who has been invited to lengthen the ecclesiastical DNA of the given family.

Now when "Jackie" first comes to the family, he (or she) is not just bringing unique gifts and competencies but is also carting along a worldview that in large measure has been ethnically informed. Jackie will see things differently as he sits down at the table in his new home. Hopefully Jackie has been knighted to bring light to the unpleasant archaeological traits laying hidden under the soil of a once homogenous community. But beware, once he begins to ask questions about why they do things the way they do and to offer suggestions, this will likely trigger the fight-or-flight impulse.

The flight response happens when Jackie makes suggestions about the worship, in the hope that it will bring more people like him into the family. The worship leader and staff will listen patiently and maybe nod their heads in outward affirmation, but often that's as far as it goes. The same will hold true for other suggestions Jackie makes.

But little does Jackie know that the people he is working with don't really want him to substantively change things (in most cases). For them, Jackie is more like a pair of red bottom shoes—a status symbol to parade around in front of other colleagues, letting them know *how serious* they are about diversity and reconciliation. But show me any Jackie on any staff who has not been legitimately heard and whose offerings have not been integrated, at least in part, and I will show you that what you really have is a token—a pair of red bottom shoes.

Even more disheartening is what happens when Jackie isn't actively seeking to bring organizational disequilibrium but is just being who he is. When Jackie stands to preach, he will often unleash the Word encased in its ethnic trappings. His intonations and cadence may carry an accented lilt unfamiliar to the ears of this fellowship of differents. The material applications that were a necessity for his tribal siblings may get him pegged as a prosperity preacher in his new home.

Don't forget, though, that God *does* bless us comprehensively, and some of those blessings *are* material; after all, "every good and perfect gift is from above" (James 1:17). This includes jobs, good health, money, and so forth. Some have erroneously branded preachers as prosperity oriented when they talk about the material blessings of God. It's only prosperity theology when the blessings become the ends and God becomes the means or the facilitator to these things. That's wrong.

How Jackie and his spouse express themselves in worship may jolt the norms of their new community. And the patriarchal view of leadership he grew accustomed to may leave him feeling disrespected by those who do not reciprocate and force him down a one-way street of contextualization. All these and more will inevitably cause some to discreetly arise from the table of *koinonia* and seek the exits. As noted in the previous sections, Jackie himself may likewise excuse himself.

The good stuff of marriage—the gravy, if you will—only emerges when we strap in and embrace one another over the long haul. When a couple says, "I do," they have no real clue what lies ahead. Korie and I never saw the miscarriages, rare diseases, sudden moves, and rebellion that make up the necessary terrain of two becoming one. Nor could we truly imagine the mundane irritants of our own idiosyncrasies we each had coddled over a lifetime of singleness. I am a morning person who squeezes the toothpaste from the bottom up and has a higher threshold for clutter. Korie is a night owl whose alarm simply signals an extra hour of sleep, who approaches the toothpaste randomly and oversees the cleanliness of the house with a white-gloved obsession. We each have a different theology of the toilet seat.

These of course just make up a modicum of the list and have caused more than a few marital realignment sessions. Yet over the decades of being together, I have learned to relax over the toothpaste and Korie over the clutter . . . somewhat. Oh yes, we have learned that more than accomplishing tasks, marriage has accomplished us. This is the gravy, the secret sauce, of marriage and relationships.

To get here we had to joyfully embrace three realities. The first is *we are different*, and the goal of marriage is never to clone one into the other's image. But we also had to abdicate any messianic delusions that somehow we were the fourth member of the Trinity called to change one another. That is an impossibility. *We can't change the other person;*

we can't even change ourselves. Only God can. The sooner we arrive at this conclusion the better we will be for it. Finally, *we had to embrace the covenant of marriage.* We were called to journey with one another for a lifetime. These three pillars of marriage are not sequential, but in some way together they form a triad of tension, making us better people.

Employment is certainly not on a par with holy matrimony, and yet it should be ventured into with a much more sobering weight than seeing it merely as some gig that affords me the opportunity of status and provision. I'm speaking, of course, within the realm of the church, though certainly this is a helpful insight for any industry. As Os Guinness reminds us in his book *The Call*, the Christian worldview is one of vocation and not merely a job,[30] and therefore it strips the employer of any utilitarian notions about Jackie. In the church, we should be at the forefront of modeling to the world how our vocational ministers are not just an amalgamation of skills, but are people—people to learn from and be bettered by, and vice versa. For Jackie or his employers (or anyone else) to pull the emergency brake and leave prematurely is to rob everyone within the community of the blessing that can only come with the collision of differents.

We once purchased a home where after six months we noticed small cracks in one of the walls. Alarmed, we called a contractor to assess things, bracing ourselves for horrific news. After some inspection we were amazed at his conclusions. The home was brand-new (the previous original owners had only lived in it for a few months before work called them elsewhere) and still settling into the foundation. It was therefore "quite common and normal" for cracks like these to appear as the house went through the process of settling in.

Genuine diversity, which flies at a higher altitude than a silence hijacked by political correctness, is messy as divergent groups settle in with one another. Ask the apostle Paul. He had to have been beyond frustrated as he inked numerous passages about matters of food to the multiethnic congregations he birthed. These were but mere cracks in their multiethnic homes. Yet Jackie and all parties must commit to seeing it through, to settling in, if you will. White evangelicalism will not expire at the hands of some sudden event or hire. Its death is more in the ilk of some slow, methodical, intentional eating away at its infrastructure. Hiring and settling in with Jackie is painful, with the zenith of its pain peaking right before the beauty of resting in the reality that we really are different, and then embracing those differences, all tethered by what Dr. Martin Luther King Jr. called "an inescapable network of mutuality."[31]

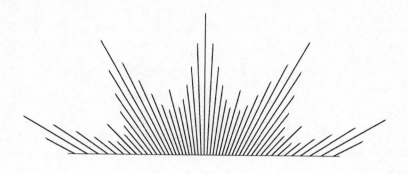

Trumped

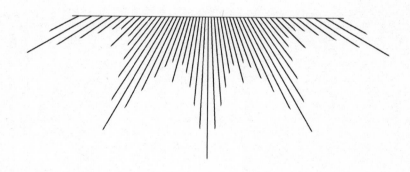

CHAPTER 27

Real Talk about
Politics and Power

Politics is a touchy issue for just about everyone. In my years as a pastor, I've seen some of the most sedate Christians passionately articulate their political convictions in a way that outpaces anything else in their lives. I've seen people who profess to be followers of Jesus Christ join a political party but not join a local church, letting it slip, by their example, where their hope truly lies. I could feel the intensity in one of my member's Facebook comments on a particular political issue, wondering why this same person stands stoically during worship as we sing praises to the King of kings. I have often been overwhelmed with a godly jealousy for the sheep of my flock whose rivers of political zeal swell as I long to dam up these waters and reroute them toward the kingdom of heaven.

It would be easy for me to walk briskly past this subject, the way I do when I'm with one of my sons in the mall and see Victoria's Secret looming a few stores down. I could divert your eyes across the way to other enticing subjects tied to white evangelicalism, but nothing quite gets at the heart of things like race and politics. And it's important for our white siblings to know why, in the late fall of 2008, many black Christians exchanged muted high-fives and chest bumps, the way we did when the O. J. Simpson verdict was read, because we knew we were in someone else's stadium, on the visiting team. So we had to keep things down when in mixed company and hold our tongue. You tend to do these things when you're not really at home.

Now, I know I'm making some of you a bit queasy, so it's important that I show you my hand. Both of them. I'm a registered independent who hates partisan politics. I've never gone to the voting booth convinced that a particular candidate will uphold all of my convictions. I voted for Barack Obama in 2008 because I as a black man was excited about the possibility of change. I didn't vote for him in 2012 because I was gravely disappointed in his policies. And I have bemoaned to my middle-class African-American tribe of friends how Obama did far more for our friends in the gay community than for us, his ethnic kin. We expected him to be God in some ways, and no mortal can ever play that role. We just aren't designed to bear the crushing weight of deity.

I've been pleading in these pages for the death of white evangelicalism because of the way she abuses power. White evangelicalism elevates the power of her limited perspective as a historical litmus test to vet the veracity of one's faith. White evangelicalism has never played well, because she will only play with others by *her* rules. If she cannot sit at the head of the table, she won't sit at all. She won't even come into the house.

Ideology is the best way to describe white evangelicalism. Tim Keller wrote, "An ideology, like an idol, is a limited, partial account of reality that is raised to the level of the final word on things."[32] This is important, for it helps us to see ideology as a concoction of perspective and power. The ideologue is never satisfied with the submission of their opinion as merely one to consider in a buffet of many, but it must be infused with a sense of power that seeks to coerce people into its image.

Ideology, Keller would go on to argue, is etymologically related to the word *idolatry*. As we know, idols are things we turn to for identity, meaning, and value. They are poor substitutes for what God seeks to be and what he offers in our lives. Idols take good things and make them ultimate things.

Politics has become for many an idol in our culture. There are several guaranteed ways to exhume the idols of our hearts, but one must ask what disproportionately triggers your emotions. If something brings you more euphoria than Jesus, it's probably an idol. If something depletes you of your joy, it's probably an idol. When I find myself being more devastated over the victory of Donald Trump than the sin in my own heart, I've just placed my finger on the pulse of my idol. And if my political party wins and I express more elation and happiness over this than over the victory won by Jesus Christ, I've discovered my idol. If I give more money to a political party than to the kingdom of God (those two things should not be confused, by the way), I've unearthed my idol.

These things must be said as we set out together to get our arms around politics and white evangelicalism. You will get frustrated, maybe even angry, and I hope it's not because I'm being careless or a bit too frivolous with my thoughts or opinions. But our visceral reactions to these matters should at least push us to pause and contemplate the question, "Has politics become our idol?"

CHAPTER 28

Squaring with the History of How We Got Here

Unless our name is God the Father or Jesus Christ or the Holy Spirit, we must have the intellectual integrity to confess that ours is a limited perspective lacking any semblance of omniscience. The way we see things is the way we see things and not how they actually are in total.

Politics is a sport played by the subjective, and it takes a huge dose of moral humility to fully embrace this. If you grew up poor and are still frantically paddling your feet under a sea of poverty to maintain some semblance of life, then this will play out in how you approach the ballot box. If, however, you grew up poor and have climbed out of the sea, only to rest your feet firmly on the land of stability and achievement, then this will hold sway over how you see things and how you cast your vote. The same can be said for those who have always been affluent and so on.

It was Lyndon Johnson's character in the movie *Selma* who insightfully told Martin Luther King Jr. that while King was an activist narrowly focused on a singular issue, Johnson was a politician whose job required a democratic "attention deficit disorder" to the host of unending issues cascading his way. This may not have been historically accurate, but embedded in this scene is a truth we can all benefit from.

Many voters approach the political process with an activist mindset. We tend to care about one note, when our country needs a symphony to keep us calibrated. It is here where as a black man, I must remember that not everything comes down to race, nor does race always rise to the top as the most urgent matter in the halls of our nation's capital. My children have brought pressing matters to their mother and me—like a desire for a certain outfit or permission to attend an event—but they do so devoid of a broader context where financial considerations and familial obligations are also pressing. Our pleas for patience and our momentary denials do not always betray our hearts.

But ours is a democracy in which the candidate for the highest office in the land is elected by the majority voice of a collective people, all electoral college disputes aside. The president of the United States occupies an office because the people have said so. And in the most shocking election in our nation's history, the people decided to install Donald J. Trump as president, and a formidable part of his base was made up of conservative white evangelicals. Statistics show that 81 percent of white evangelicals voted for him in 2016.[33] How was it that Bible-believing, white evangelical Christians chose to vote for a man who has been married three times, has bragged about sexual assault, and is generally regarded as a man of low character?

The answer to this question is a lot more nuanced than meets the eye. To be fair, many white evangelicals went to the voting booth holding their noses as they made their selection, opting for party over person. And since we are having a truth encounter, it should be noted when President Trump walked into the Oval Office, he didn't cross a sterile threshold. Many a philanderer has sat in the seat that is now his, even choosing to abuse their power in order to do their dirt. But what's different about Trump is that he seems to possess a Gotti-esque trait about him, making him the Teflon Don to whom nothing sticks. We discovered the indiscretions of Franklin Roosevelt and John Kennedy long after they met their demise. Not so with Trump. His metaphorical Carfax report was conspicuous, and we bought him as is, with white evangelicals supplying a major portion of the down payment.

If we perused an electoral map for the year 1956, we would see that almost the entire South voted Democrat. A few decades later, in 1980, most of those same Southern states had swung Republican. In one generation, the South was transformed. Of course, we understand that a major reason for this was the civil rights movement, which garnered the political support of President Lyndon Johnson, who signed the historic Civil Rights Act of 1964 and Voting Rights Act of 1965.

I need to tread lightly here, because President Johnson need not be worshiped for his love of civil rights. William Wilberforce he was not. He used the N word more than the homies on the corner, but that's neither here nor there. He outwardly did the right thing, which ended up alienating many church-attending Christians in the South and provoking one of the swiftest political metamorphoses our country has ever seen. Southern whites—many of whom were affiliated with evangelical Christianity (though can we really call them *evangelical* if there is no real push for justice?)—jumped ship and became Republicans. Some even went on to start their own private schools in an attempt to thumb their noses at government-mandated school integration. And thus a political movement began to galvanize.

The 1970s brought us Roe *v.* Wade, the tragic, landmark Supreme Court ruling legalizing abortion. It is here that the Moral Majority began to rise to national prominence, putting on a full-court press with its agenda to bring America back to God. The face of the Moral Majority was always predominantly white evangelicals. Men like D. James Kennedy, James Dobson, and Jerry Falwell were unrelenting in their stance. They got Ronald Reagan into office and began to fan the embers of a restless base. They inspired marches that protested abortion, and they hurled hateful obscenities at our friends in the gay community. It was the Moral Majority that viciously attacked the immorality of Bill Clinton, and in an irony stuffed with hypocrisy, their progeny turned around and voted for Donald Trump.

Ultimately, their legalistic fundamentalism would prove their undoing. The Moral Majority imploded, with people like Philip Yancey more than happy to offer a eulogy, which he did in his classic tome *What's So Amazing About Grace?* Sadly, she died with a lot of kids, and those kids picked up right where their parents left off.

CHAPTER 29

Is This an "Us" Space?

When our children were little, I once found myself so burdened by the historical deficiencies of their education that I thought I'd catch them up to speed by showing them the award-winning film *Eyes on the Prize*. Not the best idea in the world, because later on that evening, our youngest son, Jaden, pounded on our door, jolting us out of our sleep, convinced that members of the KKK were hiding in his closet. In Pauline terms, this is the classic case of me having zeal without knowledge.

Although I graduated from high school having fulfilled all of the academic requirements, my education felt incomplete. There were significant gaps in my American history courses. I never learned about Malcolm X or Marcus Garvey. There may have been a paragraph reserved for Dr. Martin Luther King Jr. and the civil rights movement. I didn't know about the poet Phillis Wheatley until my adult years. The same can be said for Angela Davis, and a host of other minorities. But I learned tons about George Washington and Thomas Jefferson, even though it would take years for me to discover that the cherry tree thing probably didn't happen and that Jefferson had a thing for sistahs.

But we did take field trips to Stone Mountain, where my black friends and I had to endure the climactic laser show where General Lee and the other leaders of the Confederacy came to life, riding on their laser-inspired horses while intoxicated rednecks hooted and hollered, and I left feeling the way Jaden would feel some years later.

There's an old African proverb that says that until the lion tells his side of the story, the tale of the hunt will always glorify the hunter. This is the narrative of American history, and if you don't believe it, just take a look at the words on Donald Trump's hat during the election: "Make America Great Again."

Now, I'd have no problem if the hat just read, "Make America Great," but it's the last word that sort of makes me itch. *Again?* Exactly when are you thinking? 1753? 1853? 1953? Because none of those years are good for me. I'd like a little clarity. Every time I saw Trump and his supporters' red hats, I would think back to Tom Brokaw's award-winning book on the generation that served in World War II—you know, the one he called "the greatest generation."[34] These men and women certainly should be applauded for their sacrifice. But let's keep in mind they were also a part of a generation that allowed segregation and ripped Japanese men and women out of their homes and forced them into internment camps. What Brokaw and Trump let slip is their myopic view of history, seen only from the hunter's—or white's—perch. I'm all for making America great, I'm just not for the "again" part, because while it may have been great back then for whites, that wasn't the case for people of color.

Yet there is also something insidious stitched into those four words. Donald Trump's presidency, of course, comes on the heels of that of the first African American to have ever held that office—Barack Obama. For many years, Trump nipped at the heels of Obama, questioning the authenticity of his origin of birth, thus igniting what's been called "the birther movement." Such persistent questions are laced with racist overtones, and it is against this backdrop that Trump emerged as a political candidate championing the message of making America great again. Given this, it is impossible not to hear a clarion call to place America back into white hands. Black folks had been running things for too long, and Obama's lease was now up.

I remember the angst that white evangelicals felt when Bill Clinton came into office. They were appalled by his immorality and his politics. Clinton's support of a woman's right to choose had crossed the line of demarcation. Like Obama, Clinton served his full two terms, and yes, evangelicals were elated when George W. Bush succeeded him, but the election of 2000 was not marked by the kind of palpable anger and vindictiveness we saw in the election of 2016.

But what had Barack Obama done? He was a loving husband and father. There was no Monica Lewinsky scandal. He always talked in measured tones and exercised a measure of diplomacy fit for the office. Yes, to some degree the anger was over some of his legislative agenda, but the depth of anger did not seem to fit "the crime." No other reason will fully suffice but to say that for the majority of whites, their anger stemmed from a disequilibrium brought on by the fact that for the first time in their lives, they felt like a guest in what they thought was a home they held the deed to. So as you can see, to far too many, it was time to "make America great again."

I have a Dominican friend named Robert. He's a preacher who likes to salsa, and he is passionate about diversity. We were once in a meeting with a large number of leaders trying to discern what a partnership together might look like nationally. The white facilitator was excited to share his thoughts, and we all listened patiently. Then my friend Robert interjected a question that jolted the room: "Is this an 'us' space?" Robert asked. What Robert was curious about was whether this was a place where he was going to just be a guest in the home of white evangelicalism, or whether we were sitting in a circle together with no head—in a space of mutuality. *Is this an "us" space?*

The donning of the "Make America Great Again" hats by Donald Trump and white evangelicals communicates loudly that this indeed is *not* an "us" space. What many people of color hear when they see or hear those words is an attempt to get back to a time when whites were in power and minorities were disempowered. These four words glorify the hunter and eviscerate the lion.

CHAPTER 30

A Jesus Who Can Sympathize

I was standing in line at a local restaurant waiting to order food for Jaden and me. It was the height of the lunch hour. The joint was packed, and we were hungry. Right behind me, I heard a woman in a light, lilting Spanish accent say something about white privilege. She said it in an annoyed, accusatory kind of way—the way an athlete talks to a ref whom he feels has just wronged him by calling a foul he didn't think he deserved. Everything around us seemed to stop, and when I strained to get my ear hustle on, I heard a man simply respond to her protestations by declaring loudly for the dozens of us in line to hear, "Yes, I indeed voted for Donald Trump, and the country is going to get back to where it should be." Well, okay then.

Now I'm not sure as to the exact details of this incident, but it seems as if this young twentysomething-year-old man had skipped in front of her in line—or at least that's what she perceived—which prompted her to accuse him of white privilege, which then led him to announce to all of Panera Bread that he had voted for Donald Trump. Makes total sense, I know, especially when you consider he said this in Silicon Valley, which isn't exactly home field advantage for Team Trump. He's lucky he didn't get punched in the mouth.

The scene occupied the spaces of my mind for the next several hours—a Hispanic woman holding a baby, with a toddler clutching her pant leg and looking up with an expression of fear at the young millennial who was talking in abrasive tones. I was bothered. Something was missing for me. I didn't feel like it was justified to label him a racist on the basis of this one incident, but it wasn't until I rehearsed it with Korie later that afternoon that I was finally able to make sense of it all. This man lacked sympathy, a character trait he seems to share with the man he voted for.

Much has been made of the origins of the word *sympathy*. Its etymological roots convey the ability to "suffer with." Yet through the years, the word has been cheapened, like a car with too much mileage. Overuse tends to attack the etymological equity of language and thereby depreciate its value.

The story is told of the time when the famed Beethoven was made aware of the sudden passing of a beloved friend. Though he wasn't especially known as a person of sympathy, Beethoven felt as if he had to do something. As the mourners gathered in the small home to express their grief, the door opened and in walked this musical savant. Without saying a word, he simply took his place at the piano, and for the next several hours, he played as the tears cascaded off his face and onto the keys. When the final note was played, he got up from the piano and exited the premises, never once having said a word. And yet his mere presence, along with the raw vulnerability of his gifts, communicated a profound sense of "I am with you in this moment." Beethoven expressed sympathy.

For most people of color, their time in America has been a frantic quest for dignity. This has been the story of the African diaspora's journey from day one. It bears repeating that this is why the traditional black church has insisted on attaching titles to those who serve in just about any capacity within its walls. It's also why for years in the traditional black church we dressed up, putting on our Sunday best. Our insistence on titles and church hats was not an attempt on our part to work out any perceived low self-esteem issues as much as it was a defiant shaking of the fist to a world that had tried its best during the week to bankrupt us of our dignity.

In the summer of 2016, our family landed in what is affectionately referred to as "The Bay." The journey from Memphis to the Upper West Side of Manhattan and then to Northern California was both long and breathtakingly quick all at once. Yet here we were. Not long after our arrival, I found myself in the heart of San Francisco's Fillmore District, known at one time as the Harlem of the West given its preponderance of black folk. Yet in an explicit irony, on this day I did not encounter more than three of my people in this community. What had happened?

A better question maybe is, "How did we get there in the first place?" The Fillmore used to be a Japanese community, but everything changed on that fateful December day across the Pacific at Pearl Harbor. Hysteria reverberated through our country, as Japanese men and women were rounded up and removed from their communities and herded into internment camps as if they were subhuman.

At the same time, the African-American population in San Francisco and its surrounding regions began to expand as a whole new industry opened up, readying our nation for the global conflict of war. So black folk came to San Francisco "three on a mule." What was this so-called "bastion of progress" known as San Francisco to do? With the absence of the Japanese came the answer. African Americans were herded into the now empty Fillmore, and the Harlem of the West was born. Some years later, when the Japanese people were emancipated from their wrongful confinement, they had no home to go back to. Their homes had been given to blacks by whites. Our Japanese siblings were left with no other choice but to hit reset on their lives.

These stories are told not to induce guilt, but to remind us of the context we find ourselves in—and that this context requires the remedy of *sympathy*. The young white millennial who responded to the Hispanic mother's accusation did so thinking his encounter was merely a photo—a one-time event—not understanding that he was but a scene in the movie that is America, and that scene has a context.

If one stands amazed at how the election of Barack Obama could elicit such excitement among the masses, it can be summed up primarily in the word *sympathy*. For African Americans across the political divide, it was a comforting notion to turn on the television and see that there was now someone occupying the highest office in the land who could relate to us. For most, our elation was not because we identified with the fine points of his politics (or even the larger ones, for that matter), but because we were encouraged to know that this man could legitimately say to us, in ways no other president had, that he could relate. He could sympathize.

It was the writer of Hebrews who said of Jesus, "For we do not have a high priest who is unable to sympathize with our weaknesses, but one who in every respect has been tempted as we are, yet without sin" (Hebrews 4:15 ESV). The magnitude of this verse cannot be overstated, for the writer posits our Savior as one who at his core can identify with all of us in our crucible of struggle. To women who have been victimized by the male power structures, Jesus responds by saying, "#MeToo." To men who struggle with the physiological yearnings of their loins, Jesus nods his head in solidarity. And as a fellow incarnational minority, Jesus stands with people of color, wrapping an arm around us and knowing exactly how it feels to be belittled and pillaged of ethnic dignity.

Hebrews 4:15 offers a compelling case for the present-day relevance of the incarnation. I need this Jesus. Yes, I'm thankful for his deity, but I'm also grateful for his humanity. Jesus is God enough to have overcome his temptations and yet human enough to relate to mine. This is why Christianity is attractive to me. *We serve a Jesus who can sympathize.*

Dignity must be funded through the currency of sympathy. We tread circumspectly here, however. It is the sympathetic Jesus who must be the repository of dignity. To look to humanity to give what can only be eternally supplied and sustained through Christ is to go the way of idolatry. And yet to give humanity a pass from its call to sympathize is to commit biblical malpractice. It is a harrowing truth that hovers over the pages of Scripture, making it impossible for us to bypass its shadow: the primary way God works in this world is through other people. When God wants to feed someone, he uses people. When God wants to encourage someone, he uses people. And when God wants to inflate the souls of people depleted of dignity, he uses the sympathetic billows of other people.

These truths transcend politics. The election of President Donald Trump felt like a tremendous blow to people of color in which the wind of dignity was knocked out of them. For all of President Trump's assets and liabilities, one must admit that he is not known as a man of sympathy. The tiniest fraction of objectivity will land on this conclusion.

These are matters I had to wrestle with in my own soul during the unprecedented election night of 2016. There was an amalgamation of emotions I experienced as I sat alone in my office with the state-by-state election results slowly coming in. I felt so many things, and yet it was hard to find at first a unifying theme, a common denominator. It was as if I was a little child seated at a restaurant and playing a game on the kids' menu—you know, the one where there is a collection of numbered dots seemingly scattered across the page. They seem so random—until you trace the crayon in sequential order, and a picture begins to emerge. That night, there were dots of emotions in me. Anger. Sadness. Despair. But it was only when I traced the proverbial crayon across them that a picture emerged for what I was really feeling and sensing—a lack of sympathy.

Donald Trump's election came in the midst of one of our country's greatest paradoxes. Our first black president occupied the office while a tidal wave of video-documented encounters occurred between the police and black men and women who would lose their lives—on camera, mind you. In the lion's share of those cases, the white police officers were exonerated. In my deep sadness, I found comfort in the fact that mine was a shared sadness, one carried by a black president. He sympathized. Those days were now over. Sympathy had been Trumped.

It is here where we emerge upon a frightening commonality that many white evangelicals share with Trump—a deficiency of sympathy toward the ethnically other. When Philando Castile's girlfriend was documenting his final moments, I found myself overwhelmed with grief, and yet the reflex reaction by many white evangelicals was to make an appeal for the facts or to regurgitate black-on-black crime statistics, which is, of course, misleading. White-on-white crime is just as high, which means we typically violate people we are in close geographical proximity to. White evangelicals seem to have earned a PhD in statistics, but they're at a third-grade level when it comes to sympathy.

What will it take to jerk our sympathy muscles out of their atrophying state? Hebrews 4 offers us a path forward. Jesus was never deficient when it came to sympathy, and yet the author links his sympathy to the incarnation. Jesus sympathized after he took on flesh and experienced firsthand the struggles that are common to all of humanity. It took Jesus moving into the zip code of our everydayness for him to be able to identify in the most humane way with our experience. But if Jesus was going to get the dirt of humanity under his fingernails, he had to voluntarily set aside certain dimensions of his divine privilege, because privilege can be an impediment to sympathy.

There is no hope for true sympathy if one has not been intentionally incarnational, living among the other. As long as they are issues and not people with a pulse, a story, a lived humanity, there will be no sympathy. If one only knows the ethnically other primarily through stereotypes, there is no hope for sympathy. We must incarnate ourselves in each other's skin and stories, as best we can, if biblical sympathy is going to happen. This goes for white evangelicals with people of color, and people of color with white evangelicals. Sympathy is the way of Jesus.

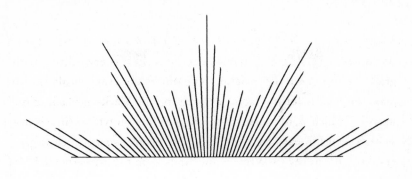

"Gay" and
Other Labels

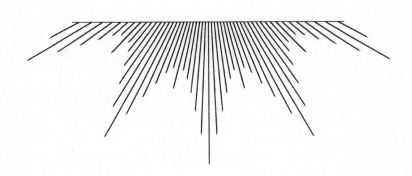

CHAPTER 31

Let's Do Better Than "Love the Sinner, Hate the Sin"

Not long after we moved to the Bay, we began looking for a team for my youngest son, Jaden, to play on. When it comes to basketball, my son is good. No, I'm serious, like effortlessly good. I know I'm a dad and I'm supposed to say it, but I really do mean it. Around our home, we call Jaden "RP"—retirement plan. I'm keeping a running tab on everything I'm spending, so when he makes it to the NBA . . . Naw, I'm just playing, sort of.

So J makes this traveling team, and we are really excited as we settle into our seats to watch his first game next to two women who are obviously a couple. As our kids run up and down the court, I find myself stealing glimpses of their affection. No, they're not affectionate in a "we just started dating a few weeks ago" kind of way. It's more like the worn affection of a couple who has broken through the intoxicant of first love, gotten over the "I hate you because I didn't know that about you," and has now settled into the "we're really in this for the long haul." We make introductions while the alarm systems are going off in me that what they're doing is not right, and I feel so stinking uncomfortable because I grew up in the Deep South, a child of the eighties.

Back in the day, being gay wasn't cool in Atlanta. Have you been to Atlanta lately? Let's just say thangs done changed, and the Atlanta of today is not the Atlanta I grew up in. "Gay" wasn't called "gay" when I was coming up. We used other names. Reprehensible names. Names that make me cringe. People who identified as gay were not people to be loved but to be laughed at because we really did think them queer.

My time in Bible college didn't confront my homophobia; in many ways it entrenched it through its passivity. The biblical training I received left no doubt that gays were more sinners than people. We were taught to love the sinner while hating the sin, with more time spent on the latter than the former. Gays were to be rejected, never to be a part of a church I pastored. On any level. This was an open-and-shut case, and for many years it was, until I sat down next to a man named Tom.

We were minutes from pulling away from the gate at LAX, and the seat next to me was empty. An empty seat next to an introvert like myself is more than an answer to prayer, especially on the long flight from Los Angeles to Memphis (where I was living at the time). But wouldn't you know it, at literally the last minute, he came running in. Sweat was pouring down his face as if he had sprinted from his house in the San Fernando Valley all the way to Inglewood on the 405. After shaking my disappointment-filled hand, he announced that he was a full-time stay-at-home dad, married to another man, and the proud father of four children he and his partner had adopted. Sprinkled in for good measure were a few f-bombs, and, of course, some moments later he asked me, a pastor, what I did for a living. The next three hours and twenty minutes were going to be interesting.

He had grown up in Memphis and was returning to look after his brother, who happened to be gay as well and had gotten into some financial trouble. I couldn't resist. I asked Tom (a made-up name) what it was like to be gay growing up in a Deep South town like Memphis, where that lifestyle is still frowned upon. I found his story to be a fascinating one—a tale filled with rejection by the evangelical church, dismissal from a parachurch ministry, and alienation from his own parents. He literally had to flee to Southern California to feel as if he could be himself.

My constant questioning of Tom definitely caught him off guard. I think he was readying himself for me to toss a few Leviticus 18 and Romans 1 grenades his way. Instead, what he got was what society would label as a conservative pastor from Memphis sincerely interested in his life and journey. I just couldn't stop. I wanted to learn more. What was his husband like? Where did they adopt their kids from? Did the kids get picked on for having two dads? Did he think any of them would embrace his same lifestyle?

And I also wanted to know what he thought about Louie Giglio being pressured by his community to not give the benediction at President Obama's second inauguration—an invitation extended by the White House. Now he was frustrated with me. "Do you think the liberal left speaks for me?" Then slowly for emphasis: "They. Do. Not." After adding that the legalistic right didn't speak for him either, he shocked me by saying that Pastor Giglio, in his opinion, should have prayed. Tom exhaled, "And who does the gay community think they are by demanding that everyone agree with them?" I sat there in silence, my assumptions dismantled.

As the plane prepared to touch down, he asked me for my contact info. Tom wanted to stay in touch. His brother attends church regularly but doesn't feel comfortable with his latest stop. "Maybe your church will be the place for him," Tom said as he pulled out his business card and scribbled his cell number across it.

I couldn't stop thinking about Tom as I lay in bed that night. In my younger days, Tom wouldn't have been Tom, an actual person; he would have been a label. Gay guy. The problem. Enemy. And where I come from, some hateful terms would have come to mind, if not rolled off my lips. But as I thought of Tom, I saw a person, a story. I felt his sense of displacement. I tried to put myself in his shoes—a thirteen-year-old boy who just felt naturally attracted to other boys, standing in the locker room, knowing he could never let on. I tried to feel his sexual disequilibrium as he walked through the halls of Rhodes College as a student in the early 1980s, telling himself that no one could know the real him or he would lose his scholarship (or so he thought). Tom was not a label to me; he was a real person made in the image of God. He was not an issue to be debated, but a person to be loved.

Moments away from sleep that night, I saw the seat next to me on the plane that for so long had sat empty, vacant. Just like that, it had been filled with a person I couldn't avoid, a person I had to address, a person who became a part of my life. Sadly, many in the Christian community would love it if the seats around us were vacant. We don't want to have to deal with people in the gay community, the Toms of our world. We wish they would stay in their midtowns, on their side of the tracks, so we won't have to think about them as we hide behind our pulpits and abuse them with Scriptures from a safe distance.

This isn't our future though. Gay marriage has been sanctioned across all fifty states. Gay voices are being heard in whole new ways. Tom is moving in next door to us. His kids are going to our schools and playing in our athletic leagues. We better have something more to say than "love the sinner, hate the sin."

Tom doesn't need our worn-out clichés. Tom needs the truth of the gospel message packaged in the unwavering love of the messenger. Tom needs to be invited into our homes, with his husband and kids, where a great steak and some good wine are waiting for him, prepared by people who love him enough to point him to the One who gave his life for him. God never asks us to change anyone—that's his business. We've been called to love and engage people in the way of Jesus, leaving the rest up to him.

CHAPTER 32

Friendship beyond
Tribal Lines

Whosen Jaden's first game ended and we climbed into the car
to make the long trek south on 280 to San Jose, Korie and I
agreed that our new Bay Area team was going to be our community,
with our sights set on building a friendship with Shante and Chrisette.
The first dinner was fun but awkward. Shante is a talker who can go
on forever about anything. Chrisette is a lot more measured . . . guarded.
She struck me as someone still reeling from a hurt that had attached
itself to her decades ago.

As we settled into dinner, Shante filled the air with her rumina-
tions, while Chrisette took things in, making silent assessments of our
home and family. Both held hands and occasionally ran their fingers
across each other's backs. Their public displays of affections weren't in a
"deal with it" sort of way—you know, as if they were trying to make a
statement. It was more like one couple being with a different couple at
dinner. Just as Korie and I embraced each other, so did they. "The sky
is blue. I'm with Korie. They are with each other." This was all so very
new to me. I mean we didn't even talk about being gay. We did talk
about how they met and about their wedding, but we didn't talk about
what it's like to be gay. It was just two couples having dinner, and I
didn't know what to make of things.

Growing up in the black church, I had been around gays before, but we never talked about them being gay. The black church has historically functioned as if it made an oath to itself to never get rid of its own for any reason, no matter how socially unacceptable it may be. We just never talked about it. So when I entered Bible college, I came as a blank sheet of paper, never having been biblically formed about how to engage people who were same-sex-attracted.

I never took a class in my conservative college or seminary on what the Bible teaches about being gay. Remember, these were the days of the early nineties, still a decade or so away from the seismic shift that would hit our culture with breathtaking speed. But I did catch statements here and there, all in a matter-of-fact sort of way, from my professors. "Being gay is sin. People aren't born that way but have been abused or have chosen to live this way. You can repent of being gay, just like you can repent of telling a lie." And of course, "You can't join a church if you are gay." These things were all said as if one were reading the weather report for the day—sheer statements of fact.

These apologetics against gays were buttressed by biblical arguments rooted in Leviticus 18, Romans 1, and other passages. So when I emerged from my theological training, it was "clear" what the Bible taught and how I was to answer those who were living in this lifestyle. But then I met Tom and Shante and Chrisette, and the first thing I had to come to terms with was that these people were not theological categories but individuals with real stories, hopes, dreams, and wounds. If I had any hope of engaging them, Romans 1 could not be our starting point. What was I to do? Sitting across the table from our new friends, I realized I had been ill-equipped to love them in the way of Jesus.

White evangelicalism does not have a history of playing well with others outside of its tribe. This is true not only with people of color, but also with people who identify as gay. There has always been an imperialistic air to white evangelicalism, to the point where if she cannot take over and be in charge, she won't come to the table. Yet things have swung so violently in our culture away from the conservative mores of a generation ago to more of a "progressive" posture that white evangelicalism has chosen to be silent as it relates to our gay neighbors. She could not voice much of her frustration with the Obama administration, for it stemmed from the landmark decision to legalize gay marriage. During the reign of the Moral Majority, white evangelicalism screamed at gays. Now she says nothing. Neither approach offers a tenable paradigm for Christocentric engagement. White evangelicalism had failed me again.

CHAPTER 33

Writing in the Sand

A woman caught in adultery is dragged to Jesus as he teaches in the temple (John 8.2–11). It is the early hours of the morning, and the religious leaders want to use this disheveled woman to back Jesus into a corner. I imagine they are clutching her by the hair, her face stained with tears. She's been humiliated, shamed. It's here that they query Jesus, pointing him to the law. She has sinned, and the law says she should be stoned. They want to know what Jesus has to say about this.

This is one of the more notable scenes in Jesus' life, for what he does next—he bends down and starts writing in the sand. In his writing, Jesus refuses to be boxed in by their either/or categories. He never satisfies their questions with a yes or no response. He simply says, "Let any one of you who is without sin be the first to throw a stone at her." Slowly they leave.

Things are never as simplistic as they seem. It may be easy to label people's actions, but it's impossible to categorize their stories. Jesus knew this woman's story, just as he knew theirs. No one had earned the right to judge this woman. What we believe is a lot easier to assemble than how we actually put those beliefs in motion.

Korie and I logged a lot of hours with Chrisette and Shante over the ensuing months following our inaugural dinner. We picked their son up and took him to practices, laughed with them late at night, and absorbed more games in the stands with one another. Their son slept over on Saturday nights after games and came to church with us on Sunday mornings. We were becoming friends.

A few months into the new spring basketball season, Shante called us. She told us that her biological son who was on Jaden's basketball team was getting to the age where he needed a positive male role model in his life, and she and Chrisette felt like it was me. So, she announced, they had decided to move from their home to a new one in our neighborhood. Of course, there would be no pressure to spend time with him, she said. They just wanted us to know. As a man who makes his living with words, I didn't have much to say. I was honored.

I began to feel guilty. Here we were, well into a friendship and they didn't know what I did for a living or what I had been taught about their lifestyle. They had no clue about the dissonance I felt. It was as if I had been carrying on an affair while keeping the whole sordid thing from my wife. Wasn't I supposed to tell them something?

Korie and I loved their son, so it was a no-brainer that we asked his moms if it'd be okay for him to go on vacation with us over the summer. This was no light request. We were going to New York for a week and then on to a Christian camp down south. When we made the pitch, we told them we'd pay for everything, and if they needed to say no, that would be fine. We told them we'd even send them the link to the camp to check it out, assuming they'd be nervous to expose him to a large gathering of Christians.

Without blinking, they agreed, and off we went. The last night of camp, their son asked me how to become a Christian, and in a walk down a well-lit path, I led him to faith in Jesus Christ. We got him a new Bible, and I promised to show him what it means to have a relationship with God.

Not long after we came home, his mother called. She said she wasn't sure about what had happened on the trip, but since her son got back, he had been carrying around his Bible and saying how she and Chrisette needed to go to church. They asked if they could come. I told them, "Of course," and invited them to sit next to us in the front row. I may have said it in more of a sedate, matter-of-fact sort of way, but I was nervous.

CHAPTER 34

Annual Women's Tea

W hile all of this was happening with Chrisette and Shante and their son, our annual women's tea—our biggest women's event—took place. Whatever image may have come to mind when I said "women's tea" is the right one. It's a formal event, the kind one wears her mother's pearls to and gets all dressed up. Our fellowship hall is filled to capacity as women eat finger sandwiches and sip tea.

So imagine one table's surprise when during the "get to know you" part, a couple announced how much they have loved being covenant partners at our church—and oh by the way, these two women, like Chrisette and Shante, are married. Talk about a record-scratching, party-halting moment. My phone buzzed for hours, as people wanted to know when I decided to allow gays to join our church. I must have explained more than a dozen times that we had not arrived at such a decision, and no, we didn't know a gay couple had joined our church. I mean, we do ask during our covenant partners class if you're single or married, but we don't ask if you are in a heterosexual or gay marriage.

I came away from these exchanges asking why they couldn't join our church. This question led to harder ones: If I did think gay marriage was wrong, then what did repentance look like? Divorce? I imagined myself saying to them, "We'd love to have you, but break up first and then you can join us." Or what if what they had testified to was true—that they were Jesus-loving people who identified as Christians?

So is it then possible to be a member of the kingdom of God but not a member of a local church? Or was the real challenge not their marriage, but what is traditionally called "church membership"? Does a person have to believe before they belong? I know I'm being a noisy thinker right now, but these matters were never a part of my formal theological training.

As I was sorting these things out, Shante stopped by our home to pick up her son. She was going on about something when she suddenly jumped subjects and asked me to officiate her and Chrisette's special vows renewal ceremony. By now she had found out I was a pastor. Chrisette didn't take the revelation well at first, feeling as if I had betrayed her. It was becoming clear that a lot of her hurt had come from Christians. I remember her actually getting up from the table and making her way to the door abruptly when she found out I was a pastor. I wanted to say, "And you call *Christians* judgmental and intolerant?" But I didn't.

I stopped Shante and asked if she ever felt judged or condemned by me. "Of course not," she said. I then asked if she felt we could be friends without agreeing on everything. "What I really want to know, Shante, is if I can disagree with you on something without being labeled a bigot?" She laughed and accused me of being dramatic. She said she knew she was making a big ask when she invited me to officiate their ceremony and figured I wouldn't be able to do it. Then, just like that, she made her way to the door and asked if we were still on to ride to the game together the next day. I said yes. She gave us the thumbs-up and bounced.

And that was that. No drama. No attitudes. No big back and forth. I couldn't believe it. It wasn't like she was asking me to watch their son for the weekend or walk their dogs. This was a big deal. She wanted me to officiate their vows renewal. Shante figured it would violate my core beliefs, but she remained secure in our friendship because she knew I loved her. Tolerance hadn't sabotaged our friendship. Love was too busy standing guard.

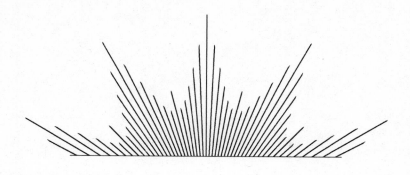

A Love Supreme

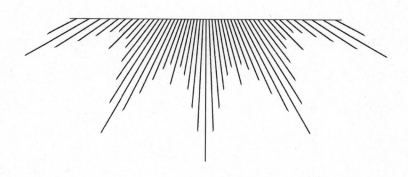

CHAPTER 35

A New Mission

I come from a tradition where creeds are louder than deeds. White evangelicalism had taught me that what I believed about Tom, Shante, and Chrisette was more important than what I actually did. Of course, it was never stated in such crass terms, and it's also a false dichotomy, because what a person really believes will be reflected by their behavior. These things notwithstanding, I had been trained to write position papers on these kinds of people but not to engage them in any sort of a way.

Things began to shift within white evangelicalism in the early 2000s. The younger generation became exhausted by the creedal lineage of our faith and sought to become more hands-on. It's here that the word *missional* crept into the evangelical lexicon. By this, they meant things like moving into impoverished communities with the aim of change. *Missional* is primarily used by white Christians who harbor messianic imaginations of saving the marginalized.

But God never calls us to be surrogate Saviors. Change is his business, not mine. Shoot, I can't even change myself. Don't get me wrong, I'm not going the way of the emerging church of yesteryear, which minimalized Christianity to tattoos, cigars, and bars, where *cool* and *community* became escape routes from doing the hard work of talking about Jesus and introducing others to him in verbal ways.

Contextualization without the punch line of the gospel leads to

161

compromise. And Lord knows I've got better things to do with my Sundays than to stand on stage and ask a whole bunch of questions, leading a community in a Q&A about Jesus. Jesus does raise questions, but he also provides answers—answers that people need.

Even if my Bible college and seminary had talked about the Toms of the world in a winsome way that equipped me to engage them well, I still would be inadequate for what they really need. I may live and articulate the gospel well, but this is not enough to save and transform them. Something was missing from my engagement with their community and with my white siblings.

The hole I was feeling led me to ask the question, "What does it mean to be Christian?" I didn't have to think long. A quick perusal of the Scriptures leads one to conclude that it's love. Jesus said the badge of the believer, what authenticates our Christianity, is not our position papers, but love (John 13:34–35). Paul wrote to the Corinthians that love is the greatest virtue (1 Corinthians 13). In talking about the fruit of the Spirit, I don't think it's any accident that the leadoff batter is love. John pulls no punches when he says, "We know that we have passed from death to life, because we love each other. Anyone who does not love remains in death" (1 John 3:14). Well, there it is.

Now this raises an important question: "What exactly does it mean to love someone?" If the authenticity of my Christianity is manifested through my love for others, then I needed to get my arms around this ethereal concept. I've settled into the notion that God has called me to be a missionary to white people, and that call means to love them. God wants me to engage Chrisette and Shante well, which means I'm called to love them. But what does this mean?

New Testament points tend to have Old Testament pictures. If 1 Corinthians 13 is the seminal New Testament text on love, then Hosea 3 is the supreme Old Testament picture of love. When someone wants to see love in real time in the Old Testament, Hosea 3 is as good as it gets.

God is frustrated when he sits down with Hosea. He has exchanged vows with Israel and entered into what the Hebrew calls *hesed* with them. *Hesed* is a unique kind of love. It's a kind of love that never gives up, gives in, or gives out. *Hesed* is a ceaseless love. One of the best English equivalents is *covenant*.

So here's God, having entered into covenant with Israel. They're married. But God is frustrated because Israel keeps cheating on him through her idolatry. God doesn't use sanitized language—he actually says they've been whoring after other gods. Now God is well within his matrimonial rights to divorce Israel because she has failed to live up to her covenantal responsibilities, but God tells Hosea he is unwilling to divorce her. He wants to stay with her and communicate to her how deeply he loves her.

Reading the blank spaces of the narrative, maybe Hosea asks what God has in mind. Maybe he wants Hosea to preach a sermon on his deep love for Israel. "Not quite," God says. Instead, God wants to use Hosea as a sort of show-and-tell to communicate his great love for his people. So he tells Hosea to marry a woman named Gomer. I can see his excitement. Maybe Hosea hits God with a litany of questions, wanting to know more about his future bride. In so many words, God tells Hosea to chill out. As Rick James would sing centuries later, "she's . . . the kind you don't take home to mother."

The opening words of Hosea 3 shed more insight into the prophet's wife: "The LORD said to me, 'Go, show your love to your wife again, though she is loved by another man and is an adulteress'" (Hosea 3:1). Earlier in the narrative, Gomer is described as being "a promiscuous woman" (Hosea 1:2). I can see Hosea's disappointment. This was not what he expected. God wants the prophet to get hitched to a prostitute. Isn't this a strange sight? The man of God with the woman of the night? But I think that's exactly the point: love is strange. After all, a holy God who is in a relationship with us sinful Gomers is even more strange. If it's never strange, I'm not sure it's ever love.

Race has done a number on the American psyche. Because of the color of a person's skin, one group of people has had their dignity inflated, while other groups have had theirs eviscerated. Given all that black people have been through in this country, it would not turn a single head if I chose to limit my community to those of the chocolate hue. But for me to initiate and revel in relationships with my historic oppressors is a strange sight to many. To be a Christian means to embrace the universal call to love, and nowhere is the mettle of love tried more than when we, in vulnerability, engage in community with those who have wounded us. I am joyfully obligated to love whites, in the same way that Jesus loved tax collectors and Roman centurions—those emblems of Jewish oppression.

For almost twenty years, my wife and I have vacationed with a tall, blond Swede named Adam and his blue-eyed wife, Nikki. We've logged hundreds of rounds of golf, sat out by fire pits, and shared hearts. When racial events happen, I can count on a call from him wanting to glean insight and understanding. Their sons jump in my arms and call me "Bluncle Bryan"—short for "Black Uncle," a suggestion of mine. They're family.

I also think of Bobby and Heather, two other dear white friends of ours. I can be a bit bourgeois when it comes to where I stay when I travel. But if I'm within a thirty-mile radius of their home in North Carolina, I call to inform them that I'm coming over for a few nights and to have my room ready. They laugh and get things situated for my arrival. Sometime that evening, we'll go out onto their big country porch and enjoy a beverage and a fine cigar, and within five minutes, the conversation takes a turn, and we find ourselves talking about things we would never share with the masses. They just have a way of pulling things out of me, these dear white Jesus lovers.

My calling to be a missionary to white people can be fatiguing. So many moments along the marathon trek, I've wanted to give up, but each time, God sends me a cup of cold water through these white friends of ours (among others), refreshing me and reminding me to stop demonizing a whole race of people. There's hope.

Not long after Shante and Chrisette moved into the neighborhood, they invited Korie and me over for their housewarming. It was a Sunday afternoon, and when Korie and I walked into the house, we quickly realized from the looks of things that we were the only heterosexual couple in the joint. This was a strange sight.

For the next several hours, we played pool and talked and laughed as a woman snapped pictures of us fraternizing with our friends and new acquaintances. We thought nothing of it as we left, but the next day, my wife texted me at the church office to inform me that we had been tagged on Facebook. *No big deal,* I thought, until a few hours later one of the sweet mothers at our church, who had to be approaching eighty, called. The moment she said she had been on Facebook, I knew where this was going. In respectful tones, she wanted to know if "I party with homosexuals"—because the Jesus she knew wouldn't do such a thing.

Now there's a verse in the Bible I don't like that says I shouldn't rebuke an older person (1 Timothy 5:1). I remembered the verse as we talked and gently offered a different way of seeing things. I encouraged her to read the gospels again and pay careful attention to the many scenes where Jesus hangs out with people whom society deemed social outcasts. We exchanged a few more cordial words and hung up. She had been offended by the "strangeness" of my relationships.

Christianity has become far too tribal. One can literally drive down a street and point to the Korean church, the rich church, the poor church, the Republican church, the Democratic church, and the white church. There's little strangeness to our relationships. We've become too normal, and the normalization of Christianity is blunting our witness to the world.

You want to turn heads? The oppressed needs to hang out with the oppressor. Japanese need to engage with Chinese, and the guy with the Obama sticker on his car should hop in the car and go to lunch with the guy who has the "Make America Great Again" sticker on his. If we have any hope of eulogizing white evangelicalism, we must drift from tribally typical to eclectically strange.

CHAPTER 36

To Be Like God

I'm not sure when it happened, but it did happen. By the time we get to Hosea 3, the prophet and the prostitute have filed for separation, and from the looks of things, she's to blame. Gomer's old proclivities seem to have gotten the best of her. If her thing was alcohol, we'd say she had fallen off the wagon. Old habits die hard, but this particular habit has gotten her in deep trouble. Chalk it up to poor choices and exploitation by evil men, and what we have is what we call in modern parlance Gomer being caught in a web of sex trafficking.

I hope this is a safe place, but I must confess if I'm Hosea, I'm feeling more than a little relieved. She would never have been my first choice—or last, for that matter. All of this was God's idea, and the only reason we got together is, well, because God kind of told me to. The news of her current predicament would lead me to pray, but that's it. Plus, Hosea knows the law, and there's a part in it that talks about what to do in situations like this. Biblically speaking, the law excuses Hosea from any compulsion toward reconciliation. She has cheated, which means he not only has the right to divorce her, but he can actually have her killed if he so chooses. In strict legalese, Hosea is free and clear.

The problem however, is that love tends to fly at a higher altitude than the law. God understands this. In his omniscience he knew this day was coming. Plus, remember that Hosea's marriage to Gomer was never really about Hosea's marriage to Gomer. This union was an illustration of God's unfathomable love toward us Gomers. So God steps in, taps Hosea on the shoulder, and says, "Go, show your love to your wife again, though she is loved by another man and is an adulteress. Love her as the LORD loves the Israelites, though they turn to other gods and love the sacred raisin cakes" (Hosea 3:1). God wants Hosea to *go again*—back to the woman who has cheated on him and hurt him.

Human relationships are adventures among flawed individuals, completely colored by sin. Therefore, any odyssey in human community will disappoint. If every time someone lets us down we choose to moonwalk away from them, setting up our little boundaries, we will never know the joys of long-term, deep, sustained friendship. Community must have the water and sunlight of *go again*. It should go without saying that there are limits to this. Surely the battered woman would be wise to not go again to the abusive man, nor the child to the abusive person, among other examples.

To go again means to open ourselves all over again to the possibility of pain. If I am to invite you into the chambers of my soul, you will be let down and wounded. I won't mean to, but it is who I am. This is the reality of friendship with me. This is the reality of friendship with you.

White evangelicals have hurt me deeply through the years. I've been called nigger by them, abandoned and conspired against by them. And yet, God wants me to go again with them. At minimum, they bear his image, and I do not have the right to turn my back on anyone God has created. I've been called to love them, not ignore or tolerate them. If white evangelicalism is to be eulogized, minorities must go the way of vulnerability and in a Golgothan sense, be willing to go again.

The impetus to heed such a herculean call is to remember the context. Hosea's marriage to Gomer is a mirror of God's marriage with us. God is not calling Hosea to do something he has not already done himself. If we are Gomer, then we are perpetual adulterers, violators of the marriage covenant to our God. And yet each day, numerous times throughout the day, God goes again with us. Every act of sin is covered by God's refusal to wipe his hands clean of us and by his delightful obligation to go again and again and again with us. This is how we know he loves us. He goes again. To be like God, we must go again with others.

CHAPTER 37

Fifteen Shekels and Barley

Hosea's response to God's call to go again is not confined to the realm of the verbal. He acts. "So I bought her for fifteen shekels of silver and about a homer and a lethek of barley" (Hosea 3:2). Commentators all point out the specificity of his payment. He pays fifteen shekels of silver, along with a homer and a lethek of barley to emancipate her. What's striking about this is that the going rate for a woman caught in Gomer's predicament was thirty shekels. That's all one needed to pay to emancipate a slave.

So why doesn't the text simply read, "So I bought her for thirty shekels"? Hosea didn't have thirty shekels. To set her free cost him all he had. I can see him now frantically searching between the cushions of his sofa, checking under the bed, and dumping loose change out of his jar. The most he could come up with in currency was fifteen shekels. So he strikes a deal. If he can supplement this with a homer and a half of barley, the auctioneer will take it. To emancipate the woman who had broken her vows and his heart put him on the brink of bankruptcy.

Love anything, and it will cost you. I have some friends who are having a hard time with their daughter. She's rebellious and hooked on drugs. Prone to lies, she frequently sneaks out at night and sleeps with men, who if they were caught would spend a long time in jail, given the youthfulness of their daughter. They have tried just about everything to get to her. Their last recourse is to send her to a rehab facility, and yet they don't make enough money to pay for it. So they're selling one of their cars and their home, taking the cash, and moving into an apartment.

I don't tell you this to make heroes out of them. Frankly, it's just the opposite. There should be a sense in which we shrug our shoulders and say, "Of course that's what parents do for their children. They love them." But this is the point. Love costs. Venture into anything beyond the trite and trivial and *really love*, and you will pay a cost. The deepest friendships have had to liquidate from their relational accounts the currency of love. Every great marriage and friendship I know has brought to the table its own fifteen shekels, plus a homer and a lethek of barley.

If love is manifested in costly sacrifice toward others, then I'm not sure white evangelicalism has ever loved me. Her refusal to put people of color in the syllabus, to integrate minorities into the power structures of her institutions, and to relinquish control to the ethnically other is exhibit A in her reticence to love in an authentic, costly way. White evangelicalism has always looked out for herself.

When churches steeped in white evangelicalism seek to hire minorities but will not infuse them with power in a way that costs and does violence to the status quo, they are not loving in the way of Hosea. To love supremely means we pull out our fifteen shekels of silver and a homer and a lethek of barley. White evangelicalism will never be eulogized by convenience. She must be crucified, just as any sin that gets between us and Christ must be crucified. For this is the way of love.

It was on the cross that God paid his fifteen shekels and a homer and a lethek of barley for us by giving up his only Son. Jesus joined in. He paid our emancipation price by offering all that he had on the cross for us Gomers.

CHAPTER 38

Raising the Bar
on Tolerance

If the narrative of Hosea 3 ended here, we would be led to think of love in an abusive way, where one becomes a doormat who accommodates to the narcissistic impulses of the other. If Hosea 3 ended after verse 2, this wouldn't really be love; it would be abuse at the hands of tolerance.

Moments after paying all that he had to redeem Gomer, Hosea looks her in her eye and says, "You are to live with me many days; you must not be a prostitute or be intimate with any man, and I will behave the same way toward you" (Hosea 3:3).

Tolerance is such a low ethic. We actually applaud people for tolerating others. It used to be that tolerance was the ability to disagree with someone else and articulate those disagreements civilly. Now tolerance has devolved into this mushy, spineless thing where we nod our heads at one another's opinions, exchanging applause for standing up for "your truth." But this is not how the Bible depicts love. Love has a standard. It has a backbone.

It may sound strange to say there's a standard or a plumb line to love, but that is exactly the case when one considers that the biblical ethic of love ultimately trespasses on, and at times even transgresses against, feelings. In his first letter to the Corinthians, Paul describes love in nonemotive terms, calling love "patient" and "kind," teaching that it "always trusts" and "always perseveres" (13:4, 7). At its height and depth, Paul reaches for just the right word when he exclaims that the volitional nature of love is something that "never fails" (13:8). Love is far more than *eros*; it has a supernatural *agape*-ness to it, which is why it requires an otherworldly animating force supplied by the Holy Spirit.

I know God loves me because he sent his Son to die for me. I know Jesus loved me because he died for me. Our friends' daughter, years from now removed from rehab, will know her parents loved her because they sold their home for her. As my friend Bob Goff says, "Love does."[35] While tolerance nods its head in passive approval, love moves to act.

But if the power of love is to be harnessed, it must move in formation, heeding a centralized command. Love—true love—needs a standard. Hosea understood this. If he and Gomer had any hopes of having a flourishing marriage, they needed core agreements mutually accepted by both parties. In my years of pastoral counseling helping couples emerge from the ashes of infidelity, I likewise understood there needed to be a love constitution, a standard of sorts. Things like a ferocious commitment to unsolicited truth, accountability, and forgiveness needed to be adhered to if this couple were to find its way out of the dark night of the soul. These are the simple mathematics of love.

We must be sure to take note of the sequence of Hosea 3. Hosea does not give Gomer the standard before he emancipates and embraces her. He doesn't say, "Hey Gomer, I've worked everything out with your captors. They'll take my fifteen shekels and a homer and a lethek of barley—which, by the way, cost me everything—but before I do that, here's what you'll need to do. If you can agree to this, then I'll accept you." Had Hosea done that, Gomer's redemption would have been predicated not on grace but on performance. Instead, he redeems and emancipates her and then gives her the standard. She is set free and accepted before she submits.

Now remember that this gives us a window into how God handles us. God doesn't set the standard and then redeem us. For example, God didn't show up to the Israelites while they were in bondage in Egypt and say, "Hey, I'd love to set you free, but before I open up the Red Sea, here's a list of commandments I need you to comply with. Do these, and then I'll see whether you're serious and I'll set you free." Instead, God opens up the Red Sea and then gives them the Ten Commandments. How did we get into relationship with God? It wasn't by works, but by grace. God redeemed us, and now our response, stimulated by grace, is that we want to give to others, serve them, and share the joy of our faith with them because God paid all that he had for us. This is love.

If I understand this correctly, then God doesn't require me to do everything correctly before he opens his arms and embraces me. Justification only requires the act of faith (given by God). He accepts us as we are. Sanctification is the long road to becoming what he has already declared us to be—that is, righteous. It is along that road where God will inevitably tap us on the shoulder and show us things sequestered in the corner of our souls that do not look like him. Yet we don't need to change before he accepts us. We can't change without him.

Seen in this light, this is where white evangelicalism becomes an affront to the gospel. If the standard of the gospel is *faith alone* in Jesus Christ—*sola fide*—and God says that's good enough for me to accept you, then to add to this standard is to stand in the lineage of the Judaizers. To not embrace another Christian because they're not in conformity to our standards is both oppressive and arrogant. To refuse to play with those deemed not gospel-centered enough or too charismatic, too justice driven, or too pro-choice is to draw lines that God doesn't draw. Yes, we all carry our own theological accents, but this should not lead us into a "linguistic oppression," forcing others to morph into our way of theological-speak before we accept them.

I'm the oldest of four children, and while my parents had some universal standards, they really did treat us differently, refusing to cookie-cutter us as if we were some new housing development on the outskirts of town designed by a lone architect. Some of us went to private schools, while others did not. Some could get by with C's and even the occasional D, while others could not. There were times I would blow the whistle and call "foul" on my parents' blatant favoritism, only to hear them say, "Fairness is not always sameness." Dad was adamant in his refusal to apply universal standards in lesser things to all of his children. That would be unfair and oppressive.

Having just completed breakfast with Jesus on a beach one day after Jesus' resurrection, Peter received some not so pleasant news. Jesus talked to him about the way he was going to die. I can see in my mind Peter pointing to John and channeling his inner child as he says to Jesus, "Lord, what about him?" (John 21:21). Jesus responds, "If I want him to remain alive until I return, what is that to you? You must follow me" (verse 22).

Fairness is not necessarily sameness. Jesus felt no inclination to apply universal standards to nonessential items. This is a trend in the Scriptures. Gentiles did not have to become Jewish to be Christian. And not every rich person had to go the way of the rich young ruler by selling everything before following Jesus. Fairness isn't sameness. The only standard that is set in stone is *faith in Christ alone.*

I had a dream the other night. My wife and I were eating dinner with the women's tea party couple who had announced their joy over joining our church. The elders had sent me on a mission to sort this out. So we spent the first thirty minutes or so finding out about their marriage—how they met, where they got married. We talked some about their relationship with Christ. They talked in convincing terms of their absolute love for the Lord.

Just then, at the table behind them, a man had his phone turned up too loud. It was obvious that he was watching something—something really inappropriate. The sounds were of a sexual nature. Disturbed, I found myself trying to appear as if I was fully engaged with the couple from our church, but I was also distracted. Finally, when I could take it no longer, I asked to be excused, rose from my seat, and walked over to this gentleman's table. Approaching him from the back, I saw a set of handcuffs around his right wrist, with a chain leading to the phone.

I caught a quick glimpse of what was pornography and looked away. Now I was really annoyed. As politely as I could, I asked him to excuse me. He turned around slowly, and when our faces met, I couldn't believe it—it was one of my elders, a man who had been a member of our church for decades. Without the slightest hint of embarrassment, he confessed to being addicted to pornography for years. I was shocked. Just then the manager of the restaurant approached us, looked at me, and asked, "Would you like us to put him out?" But I interpreted his question as if he was asking if I thought he should be removed from the church. After a moment of silence, I looked at the couple we were having dinner with and then back at him. Finally, I awoke from my dream with no resolution.

So I'm off to my meeting with this couple, and, no, it's not a dream. I need to address what is the standard for engagement, for becoming a part of the people of God in the local church. Is faith in Christ, indicated by a thirst for holiness, enough? Or do we need to add more standards? The history of evangelicalism has drifted toward a Judaizing trajectory. We must keep a firm grip on our core convictions, while we hold lightly and humbly to nonessential items. Easier said than done—and in this tension, we find our invitation.

A Hopeful Eulogy

Practical Steps to Realizing
the Desired Kingdom

If you're a fan of sports, you not only want your team to make the playoffs, but you also hold out hope that it earns what is aptly called "home field advantage." There really is no better way to say it than that—whoever plays host to the game has a decided advantage. The visiting team is at a decided disadvantage—walking into not only a different stadium but also one infused by a foreign culture that will inevitably be hostile to any movements they make as visitors on the field of play.

If, for example, you are playing against the Pittsburgh Steelers, you will encounter a sea of rabid fans waving those "terrible towels." Or if you have the misfortune of playing in Duke's Cameron Indoor Stadium, brace yourself to be tormented by those "Cameron Crazies," who have more than lived up to their name over the years. Since 1939, the Duke men's basketball team boasts a home record of 875–157, an 85 percent success rate.[36] Playing as a visitor in someone else's court, field, or stadium places one at a undeniable deficit.

Since the first European immigrants set foot in America in the 1600s, Christianity has been played in the stadium of what we now know as white evangelicalism. White evangelicalism has been the home team. Look hard enough, and many African-American Christians can trace their spiritual lineage back to whites in this country. And because theology always comes with its unique ethnic accent, most of what has been handed to us is a theology done in white.

Slavery was "justified" by white Christians because their theological accents led them to misuse biblical passages. Segregation was sustained due to a theology spoken in a white brogue. Even many of the lingering ecclesiastical and theological practices embraced by people of color are nothing more than cultural expressions or misunderstandings cloaked in white evangelicalism.

I say these things—these very hard things—not to heap guilt, but to underscore the point that the narrative of Christianity in America is one where whites have been the home team and have fielded a decided, oppressive advantage for centuries.

We continue to feel these lingering effects. If a minority pastor wants to plant a church with any hope of success, he must be able to raise money from white people. If a person of color feels called to join a nonprofit Christian organization based on a support-raising model, she must be able to solicit funds from whites. And if one wants to study the Scriptures at an institution that holds to traditional orthodoxy, they must be willing to sacrifice the ethnic dimension of their makeup and float adrift in a sea of racial anonymity—and at times hostility.

These examples reflect the reality that people of color must be able to relate well to whites, presenting themselves in palatable ways. This is not a two-way street. White people can plant churches and raise money and attend orthodox Christian schools without having to relate to us. They are the home team with all the advantages that come with it.

From the time I was a little boy, I felt like a stranger in the land of white evangelicalism. I distinctly remember times when my father would take me to hear him preach at college conferences—events that were supposed to reach major colleges and universities across a given region—and yet when I sat down, I noticed that the attendees were almost exclusively white. What's more, not one worship song sounded familiar to my ears that had been steeped in the rich gospel tradition of the black church I attended. Looking back, the only time I felt like a stranger was not when I was at school or in athletics, but in Christian environments hosted by whites.

My sojourn in Memphis reinforced these suspicions. We had no problem getting white people to check us out, but African Americans were another story—and understandably so. Leaving the African-American church is hard, due to the deep, abiding attachments to it in places like Memphis. Those few hours on Sunday morning are the rare moments where one feels like they're at home, an oasis in a week dominated by venturing into visiting stadiums like work and school. It's tiring to always play the part of a stranger. We long for home.

These are important things to excavate as we seek to develop a path forward that will give white evangelicalism its last rites. The founding carriers of Christianity were ethnic Jews. Or to say it another way, Christianity was originally spoken with a distinct Jewish accent, and this turned out to be problematic almost from the outset. In Acts 11, Jewish leaders question the validity of Peter's actions in going to "uncircumcised men" (verse 2). The volume rises in Acts 15 when the first church council is held, because all of these Gentiles are coming to faith. So more questions are asked, like, "Do they need to be circumcised?" The essence of this question (and others) had to do with whether these new non-Jewish believers needed to act Jewish in order to be really saved. Peter speaks up first, and then James follows, with a passionate *no* (Acts 15:11, 19).

This is a profound message for us. These Jewish, Jesus-loving leaders made a decision that there was to be no ethnic home team when it came to Christianity. They carefully parsed out what was gospel and what was cultural, and they gave each other the space to express themselves redemptively in nonessential matters that did not do violence to their ethnicity and culture. Reading their conclusion carefully one readily sees that the emphasis is to be on holiness, on Christlikeness, and not on ethnic or cultural practices.

The Choice to See

So what does this mean for us as we venture forward into the desired kingdom? First, Acts shows us that the only ones who have the capacity to eulogize the home field advantage of the ethnic home team are members of the ethnic home team with the home field advantage. Appeals from minorities to do this have done nothing but frustrate minorities—and whites, for that matter. The power brokers in the infancy of Christianity were Jews, and it was Jews who made the decision to eulogize "Jewish evangelicalism."

The principle here is one of *seeing* or *awareness*. Paul and Barnabas— two Jews who were members of the ethnic home team—made their fellow Jewish leaders aware of the problem. In our context, whites must see and make fellow whites aware of these things. Had Paul and Barnabas gone the passive and silent route, this book you are reading would have made an appeal for the death of "Jewish evangelicalism" and not "white evangelicalism." These Jewish Jesus lovers moved swiftly to wrest the hands of Jewishness from Christianity. The same must be true here. Whites must see and move decisively to wrest the hands of whiteness from Christianity. Silence is not an option when it comes to wiping out ethnic home field advantage.

If you're a leader of a primarily white church or organization, this presents you with some wonderfully courageous opportunities. When injustice is brought to national attention, you need to know that the people of color who come to your church or organization are crossing their fingers and silently hoping you will say something. You may not need to change your sermon or address every time to deal with the issue, but you can incorporate it into the prayer time, and you can grieve with those who grieve. If you're not a leader, you can still help people to see by creating what I call little awkward moments. So when that friend or family member says something racially insensitive around the dinner table, don't just be silent; call it out. It's not good enough to just not be racist; we must be aggressively antiracist.

The Choice to Empower

But there's more. Infused with a new sense of hope, Paul, a Jew, goes out and plants more churches, venturing further and further away from Jerusalem, and as he does, he often appoints non-Jewish leaders over these new churches. In other words, he doesn't horde power, but he gives power away to these Gentile leaders. Consider Titus, a Greek man (Galatians 2:3) who was discipled by Paul and appointed to be the pastor of the churches in Crete. Paul writes to him to give instructions for appointing elders in these churches. What is Paul doing here? He is simply empowering an ethnically different leader.

White evangelicals must seize every opportunity they can to steward their privilege well by disadvantaging themselves for the advantage of others. There should be a vision to find and empower capable and well-qualified people of color for seats in Christian higher education. As communities continue to change demographically, the next generation of Tituses should be identified, equipped, and then positioned in seats of power, matching the forecasted new ethnic demographics. If this sounds like affirmative action to you, then so be it. If by affirmative action one means profiling a specific ethnicity for certain opportunities, then this has been going on for centuries. Who could have run for president in 1860? Who could have been president of Stanford in 1950?

The Choice for Decisive Action

What Paul and the early leaders of the church model for us is an intense cross-cultural action. Here's a sure fact born out of decades of multiethnic ministry: If I want to make my white siblings angry, I should talk about race in such a way that there is a hint of culpability on their part. My Twitter feed lights up, my inbox swells, and my personal website comes dangerously close to shutting down.

Okay, there's some passion. That's good. But all things aside, let's be equitable with our passionate outbursts. I'd love to see some of that same passion bottled up and then dispensed when it comes to the shooting death of Philando Castile or the mess in Charlottesville. How can there be cries of injustice toward me in raising the issue and yet silence over dead minority bodies in the streets? These seem to be the actions of the home team.

I once served as the only person of color on the board of a very prestigious school. Now I'm not complaining about this, because you have to start somewhere, and the head of this school came across to me as a well-intentioned leader who authentically wanted to make progress in the area of diversity. But there was one problem. I soon learned that many of our board functions would take place at a restrictive country club.

I pulled him aside and told him I would not be attending any of those events at the country club for obvious reasons, quietly hoping he'd get the hint and change venues. He never did. It was then that I reached the conclusion he wanted me for the optics and not for genuine change. I soon made my exit. I learned a valuable lesson: Power and position are not always synonymous. A powerless position is a token.

But I have glimpsed moments of hope. A few years ago, I was contacted by a church that was desperate to be multiethnic and knew they had to hire a "Titus" if they had any hopes of experiencing the desired kingdom. But as they looked at their budget, they saw that their resources did not match their appetite. The white pastor was so convinced that this was what God wanted for him and his church that he gave up his pay for a year and redirected it to the new minority pastor they hired. He also made sure this new leader was his equal on the team, and he broadcast that message loudly to the church. I've never seen anything like this. He disadvantaged himself for the advantage of another. Talk about stewarding white privilege well. This is the hopeful eulogy to white evangelicalism.

The Choice to Cultivate Relationships

I've been writing and speaking on race relations for years. I've flown more than a million and a half miles crossing the globe to talk about these matters, and here's what I've concluded: We just don't know each other well. Read the comments section on any blog or social media post dealing with race, and what you're bound to discover are not only differences of opinion but also incredible hostility. Genuine multiethnic friendships are a rarity, and we are suffering because of it.

I was preaching at a Southern Presbyterian church some years ago on forgiveness. My closing illustration reflected on a person I needed to forgive for calling me a racially offensive term. As soon as I concluded, a middle-aged white man made a beeline to me. His posture was defensive. He wondered aloud why race was such a big deal to people like me. When he finished, I said, "Sir, do you have any real minority friendships?" He paused and confessed that he didn't. His resistance to living in close communal proximity with the ethnically other had allowed his empathy muscles to atrophy. I need friendships with whites to keep me from getting bitter and cynical. And whites need minority friendships to help them understand such things as systemic injustice.

But it should be said that these friendships must be genuine, and if they are, then there will be moments of robust discourse where variant viewpoints are expressed. I fear race relations, especially in conservative Christian contexts, are being hijacked by political correctness. Conflict, not political correctness, is the sign of healthy relationships. If my wife never expressed what she really thought, never offered a variant viewpoint for fear that I would reject her or think less of her, we would not diagnose our marriage as a healthy one. What makes our marriage healthy is the confidence to "go there," with one another, expressing things we honestly think and feel, knowing that it cuts against the grain of what the other thinks and feels. What gives us the confidence is an atmosphere of love where we know our spouse is not going to leave.

Christians believe the great command entails loving our neighbor. Jesus even helps us to see our neighbor as the ethnically other in his tale of the Good Samaritan (Luke 10:30–37). Love is not paralyzed by political correctness. It's not healthy for minorities to commandeer the conversation and vent while our white siblings just sit back and take it, never expressing how they feel as well. We will know we are journeying deeper into the kingdom Jesus desired—one made of people from every nation, tribe, and tongue—when some of our white friends feel so secure in that multiethnic friendship that they say, "I actually think Donald Trump is doing a great job."

A final word should be said about tribal warfare and white idolization. Acts 10 describes a defining moment for the church as Jewish Peter preaches the gospel to a gathering of Gentiles and they receive Christ. We would think this would be a moment for rejoicing, but the opening lines of Acts 11 cause us to grieve: "The apostles and the believers throughout Judea heard that the Gentiles also had received the word of God. So when Peter went up to Jerusalem, *the circumcised believers criticized him*" (Acts 11:1–2, emphasis mine).

Here we have fellow Jews lining up to condemn another Jew (Peter) for following God by taking the gospel across ethnic lines. What they desired was to have an ethnic monopoly on the gospel. We can smell the stench of prejudice as this Jewish cohort lets their displeasure be known. Unfortunately, tribal warfare like this continues today, and if we do not call attention to it, we will have no hope for dismantling white evangelicalism.

At its core is misplaced identity. Notice these men were referred to as "the circumcised." They were identified not by their faith, but by their distinctive ethnic characteristic (circumcision). Ethnic tribal warfare begins when we allow our primary identity to be found in our race and not in our Christ. When being black matters more than being Christian, or when being Korean matters more than being a follower of Jesus, we have ventured into idolatry.

There is such a thing as a "blackness that whiteness created."[37] Since the beginning of our sojourn here in America, many African Americans have unconsciously used whiteness as an identity marker for blackness. At times historically, we saw closeness to whiteness as a good thing (both in skin tone, speech, and other areas). But at the same time, there was a contingent of African Americans who saw proximity to whiteness as a deeply negative thing—and this viewpoint continues broadly today. I got accused of acting white in high school because I made good grades. The way I talk has caused other African Americans to pejoratively brand me as sounding or acting white. The fact that I pastor not a black church but a multiethnic one somehow makes me less black. Tribal warfare.

Now the irony here is that we have made whiteness a benchmark for our identity. Don't you see? To some, the closer one is to what they perceive as whiteness, the less black they actually are. And yet others believe the further one is from whiteness, the more authentically black they are. The maddening factor to all of this is that many African Americans have unwittingly empowered the very thing they want to dismantle in their identity formation—whiteness. Even more disheartening for the Christ follower is that we have relegated our identity from Christ to ethnicity.

Please don't misunderstand me. God created ethnicity. Ethnic distinctions are not a fruit of the fall. John looked into heaven and saw ethnicity (Revelation 5:9–10). The call to follow Jesus is not the call to disrobe my ethnicity. Jesus did come to earth as a Jew. I was created as a black man. I can be both genuinely Christian and redemptively black.

These things are important to discuss within the context of the appeal to dismantle white evangelicalism, because tribal warfare within ethnicities distracts us from experiencing the desired kingdom of multiethnic community. The "circumcised believers" were never going to know the joy of experiencing life with Gentiles because they were too busy idolizing their ethnicity. And the same is true when one is constantly feeling their heels nipped at by members of their own race who wonder when they're going to "come back home."

Yet the opposite—white idolization—is problematic as well. White idolization happens when their approval of us is sought more than the approval of God (1 Corinthians 4:1–5; Galatians 1:10). When I am disproportionately devastated because some well-known white speaker who hosts a primarily white conference doesn't invite me to speak or doesn't ask me to endorse his book or turns down my request to endorse

mine, then I have not only fallen into idolatry (on a par with that of ethnic tribalism), but I am facilitating a subtle form of white oppression. People of color need to be redemptively free of the approval of others as validation for who they are and for the endeavors they steward. Yes, people occupying historic positions of power need to seek opportunities to empower, but I cannot press pause on the call of God on my life in the hopes that I get noticed and called on. What God has for us no human being can thwart (Acts 5:39).

Though my journey has been exhausting at times, I'm hopeful. More multiethnic churches exist today than ten years ago. The volume is being turned up on the race conversation, with voices beginning to chime in from once unlikely places. The rising generation is marching in the streets for justice, and many of them are Jesus-loving white people. Sure, there have been missteps and we still have a long way to go, but I see God nudging us forward. And for this, I'm grateful.

Acknowledgments

My bride, Korie, is a stunningly beautiful gift to me and the body of Christ. If more people would follow her example in how she engages others, this book would not need to be written. I'm grateful to God for her.

My parents, Bishop Kenneth Ulmer, Dr. Tony Evans, Dr. Gordon Kirk, and Dr. Dennis Rainey have been significant influences in my life and thinking. I stand on their shoulders. When it comes to the hope I continue to harbor in race relations, I owe a special thanks to Gordon Kirk and Dennis Rainey. These two Jesus-loving white men came along at critical junctures in my story, often posturing themselves as learners and cheering me on.

Zondervan has been remarkable with this project. Something began to stir in me late in the fall of 2017, and I just sat down at a computer and wrote. A few weeks later, I emerged with this book. I passed it along to my agent, Andrew Wolgemuth, and to Stephanie Smith at Zondervan, wondering if they would take it on. Stephanie and the Zondervan team were significant encouragers who embraced the project and offered valuable input to my original manuscript. They've been courageously generous as a company to give me a voice to the rumblings in my soul. Thank you.

Finally, the people of Abundant Life are simply amazing. This multiethnic church I have the privilege to pastor has modeled to the world the desired outcome of a multiethnic community that deeply loves Jesus and one another. What an honor it is to serve them!

Notes

1. Mark A. Noll, *The Civil War as a Theological Crisis* (Chapel Hill: University of North Carolina Press, 2006), 52.
2. W. E. B. Du Bois, *The Souls of Black Folk* (1903; repr., New York: Dover, 1994), 2.
3. Betty Watson Burston, Dionne Jones, and Pat Robertson-Saunders, "Drug Use and African Americans: Myth Versus Reality," *Journal of Alcohol and Drug Education* 40, no. 2 (Winter 1995): 19.
4. Michelle Alexander, *The New Jim Crow: Mass Incarceration in the Age of Colorblindness* (New York: New Press, 2012), 6–7.
5. Bryan Stevenson, *Just Mercy: A Story of Justice and Redemption* (New York: Spiegel and Grau, 2014), 29.
6. Nicholas Wolterstorff, *Justice: Rights and Wrongs* (Princeton, NJ: Princeton University Press, 2010), 115.
7. Cited in Ibram X. Kendi, *Stamped from the Beginning: The Definitive History of Racist Ideas in America* (New York: Nation Books, 2016), 69.
8. See Pete Scazzero, *The Emotionally Healthy Church: A Strategy for Discipleship That Actually Changes Lives*, 2nd ed. (Grand Rapids: Zondervan, 2010), 97–101.
9. Raymond Chang, "Open Letter to John Piper on White Evangelicalism and Multiethnic Relations," *Christianity Today*, October 19, 2017, www.christianitytoday.com/edstetzer/2017/october/open-letter-to-john-piper-on-white-evangelicalism-and-multi.html.

10. See "Five Levels of Communication: Introduction," http://
    704f17d79dab7ea38deb-7e7fa4322931eaefe9e6c6026c8dd1cb.r19
    .cf2.rackcdn.com/uploaded/m/0e5153478_1465440953_marriage
    -encounter-handout-6-4-16.pdf.
11. See Dietrich Bonhoeffer, *Life Together* (New York: Harper & Row,
    1954).
12. Du Bois, *The Souls of Black Folk*, 2–3.
13. Philip Yancey, *What's So Amazing About Grace?* (Grand Rapids:
    Zondervan, 1997).
14. Charles C. Ryrie, *Dispensationalism Today* (Chicago: Moody, 1965).
15. Ryrie, *Dispensationalism Today*, 46–47.
16. See Michael O. Emerson and Christian Smith, *Divided by Faith:
    Evangelical Religion and the Problem of Race in America* (New York:
    Oxford University Press, 2000).
17. Reggie Williams, *Bonhoeffer's Black Jesus: Harlem's Renaissance
    Theology and an Ethic of Resistance* (Waco, TX: Baylor University
    Press, 2014).
18. J. D. Vance, *Hillbilly Elegy: A Memoir of a Family and Culture in Crisis*
    (New York: HarperCollins, 2016).
19. See John Piper, "God Is Always Doing 10,000 Things in Your Life,"
    Desiring God, January 1, 2013, www.desiringgod.org/articles/every
    -moment-in-2013-god-will-be-doing-10-000-things-in-your-life.
20. Korie L. Edwards, *The Elusive Dream: The Power of Race in
    Interracial Churches* (New York: Oxford University Press, 2008), 19–37.
21. See Isabel Wilkerson, *The Warmth of Other Suns: The Epic Story of
    America's Great Migration* (New York: Random House, 2010).
22. Mary Beth Swetnam Mathews, *Doctrine and Race: African American
    Evangelicals and Fundamentalism Between the Wars* (Tuscaloosa:
    University of Alabama Press, 2017).
23. See Wilkerson, *Warmth of Other Suns*, 240–41.
24. See Kay Wills Wyma, *Cleaning House: A Mom's 12-Month Exper-
    iment to Rid Her Home of Youth Entitlement* (Colorado Springs:
    Multnomah, 2012).

25. See Lawrence Otis Graham, *Our Kind of People: Inside America's Black Upper Class* (New York: HarperCollins, 1999) esp. 1–18.

26. Ja'Net Du Bois and Jeff Barry, "Movin' On Up" (Sony/ATV Music Publishing)—theme song from the TV show *The Jeffersons*.

27. Bryan Loritts, *Right Color, Wrong Culture: The Type of Leader Every Organization Needs to Become Multiethnic* (Chicago: Moody, 2014), 122.

28. Edwards, *The Elusive Dream*.

29. Scot McKnight, *A Fellowship of Differents: Showing the World God's Design for Life Together* (Grand Rapids: Zondervan, 2014).

30. Os Guinness, *The Call: Finding and Fulfilling the Central Purpose of Your Life* (Nashville: W Publishing, 2003), 36–42.

31. Martin Luther King Jr., *Why We Can't Wait* (1963; repr., New York: Penguin, 2000), 65.

32. Timothy Keller, *Counterfeit Gods: The Empty Promises of Money, Sex, and Power, and the Only Hope That Matters* (New York: Penguin, 2009), 104.

33. Stephen Mansfield, *Choosing Donald Trump: God, Anger, Hope, and Why Christian Conservatives Supported Him* (Grand Rapids: Baker, 2017), 96.

34. Tom Brokaw, *The Greatest Generation* (New York: Random House, 1998).

35. Bob Goff, *Love Does: Discover a Secretly Incredible Life in an Ordinary World* (Nashville: Nelson, 2012).

36. "Men's Division I Home Court Records," *Collegiate Basketball News*, www.rpiratings.com/homecourtrec.php.

37. Victor Anderson, *Beyond Ontological Blackness: An Essay on African American Religious and Cultural Criticism* (1995; repr. New York: Bloomsbury, 2016), 13.

Saving the Saved

How Jesus Saves Us from Try-Harder Christianity into Performance-Free Love

Bryan Loritts

God doesn't want your spiritual score-keeping; he simply wants your surrender.

You already know because you've tried. Repeated attempts to earn God's love and approval have gotten you nowhere and left you exhausted. When performance taints your relationship with God, the Christian life can turn into an unholy hustle. It was never meant to be like this.

The good news of the gospel of Matthew was a breath of fresh air—a message of grace and performance-free love—to do-better, try-harder Jews who thought they had to earn their way into God's favor.

The ancient message is a lifeline to us today too as we live in a world based on measuring performance. Just as Matthew wrote to the Jews in his gospel, we were never meant to flounder under the pressures and anxieties of show Christianity. Make no mistake: we are called to live in obedience, but Jesus wants us to save us from the illusion that our actions can ever make God love us any more or any less.

In Pastor Bryan's relevant, uncompromising style, *Saving the Saved* proclaims the good news that once the pressure is off to perform, we are free to abide. Beyond the man-made rules and the red tape, there is a God who knows you by name. Come and meet him as you've never known him before.

Available in stores and online!